rthy of the nar___ ___ _____y
, to my mind, the noblest
use of man, or more pre-
iring mind by which man
t or not, it is nevertheless
won: a struggle which can
od and all. There are al-
society founded in the love
n who do not wish to be
r the practice of freedom
who long for the comfort
authority in their own
ore comfortable still if they
authority on the lives of
ich people exist–and they
g from the earth, even the
subvert freedom will con-
t to subvert freedom con-
ng points of defense.

Champion
of a cause

Champion of a cause

Essays and addresses on
librarianship by

Archibald
MacLeish

Compiled and with an introduction by
Eva M. Goldschmidt

American Library Association
Chicago 1971

International Standard Book Number 0-8389-0091-7 (1971)

Library of Congress Catalog Card Number 70-150577

Copyright © 1971 by the American Library Association

                              Printed in the United States of America

Every American librarian worthy of
the name is today the champion of a
cause. It is, to my mind, the noblest
of all causes for it is the cause of
man, or more precisely the cause
of the inquiring mind by which man
has come to be. But noblest or not,
it is nevertheless a cause–a struggle–
not yet won: a struggle which can
never perhaps be won for good and all.
There are always in any society,
even a society founded in the love of
freedom, men and women who do not
wish to be free themselves and who
fear the practice of freedom by others
–men and women who long for the
comfort of a spiritual and intellectual
authority in their own lives and who
would feel more comfortable still if they
could also impose such an authority
on the lives of their neighbors. As long
as such people exist–and they show
no sign of disappearing from the earth,
even the American earth–the fight to
subvert freedom will continue. And
as long as the fight to subvert freedom
continues, libraries must be strong
points of defense.

Archibald MacLeish "A Tower Which Will Not Yield"

Contents

Preface

Librarianship is one of those activities which can be a job, a profession, or an art, depending on how it is practiced. If it is a job, you get paid. If it is a profession, you give it your life. If it is an art, you are David Chambers Mearns.

My case, as Hamlet's mother puts it, was "particular." I was Librarian of Congress, which is certainly a job—in some ways the best job in the federal government—but I never reached professional rank in anyone's eyes, including my own, and as for art, my commitment was elsewhere.

All of which makes this book Eva Goldschmidt has put together a very odd volume, indeed. Here is a man talking about libraries and librarianship who knew nothing of either until he found himself, at the age of forty-seven, running the largest library in the world, and who learned whatever he did learn about the librarian's task by doing what had to be done in a situation of almost constant crisis.

The so-called phony war in Europe had started before I parked my car for the first time in the space marked "Librarian," and by the time I had found my way around the collections and departments and made up my mind what had to be done, France had fallen and the inevitability of war was apparent even to America First. A threatened world war would have affected the Library of Congress under any circumstances, but under the circumstances of

1940, war's imminence was ominous indeed. For what had to be done in the Library, as I had discovered in those first few months, was to reorganize it from technical services to pay scales, and from general administration to the binding and care of books. My predecessor, Herbert Putnam, had been a great librarian, but he had run the Library like a feudal fief, and feudal fiefs had a way of hardening and solidifying in the mold.

Moreover, there was an inner crisis to match the outer. My nomination had understandably antagonized older and better qualified men already in the profession, who saw no reason why a poet should head what was, in effect, the national library, and there had been a brief but vigorous effort to persuade Mr. Roosevelt to withdraw my name or the Senate to reject it. "A shocking appointment," said the *New York Herald-Tribune* in one of Geoffrey Parson's most eloquent editorials, and a shocking appointment it seemed to many in the American Library Association. The consequence was a rather general resentment that made reorganization of the Library difficult, because the profession as a whole, though aware that something had gone wrong with catalog cards and other services emanating from Washington, was not eager to join hands with an Ishmael to put things right.

All this — the difficulties at home and the gathering crisis abroad — will explain, perhaps, the sense of urgency and strain which runs through some of these addresses and papers. It was clear to me that unless the work were done at once, it might well have to wait for another Librarian — and the terms of my predecessors had been long . . . far too long. It is only at the beginning of an administration in any field that innovation is really possible. After a certain number of years in office the perspective is gone, and, besides, a reform then is a reflection on oneself.

But urgency is not the only tone in the papers dealing with reorganization; there is also gratitude and, I hope, an increasing sense of delight in work done in common. For the professional climate cleared much more rapidly than I had any reason to hope. Keyes Metcalf, one of the great librarians of the generation, who had called me from the San Francisco convention of the American Library Association to demand that I instruct Mr. Roosevelt to withdraw my name (he did not know Mr. Roosevelt), generously agreed to serve as a consultant in the reorganization together with Quincy Mumford, the present Librarian, and other distinguished men. And Frank Keppel, of the Carnegie Foundation, who had shared Geoffrey Parson's sentiments about my nomination, gave the Library a most helpful grant which made the consultantships effective, rather than merely honorary, offices.

But what I hope will be most clearly heard in these pages is a deeper and older gratitude—the gratitude and affection due my colleagues in the Library itself. Of Mr. Putnam's many achievements the greatest was the selection of the Library of Congress staff. It is notorious in the scholarly world that the services of the Library of Congress to its users are superior to those of any other comparable institution, and the reason for the superiority is to be found in the human beings who provide those services. When I became Librarian, they were Mr. Putnam's choices, and they have maintained their quality from one library generation to another because of the influence of the original models Mr. Putnam chose. There were no finer public servants in Washington in the early forties than Verner Clapp, David Mearns, and their associates, and the few I added during my brief term—Luther Evans was one of the first—found themselves at home.

If these pages Mrs. Goldschmidt has gathered out of the past have any meaning today, it is because these men and women undertook the labor with me as freely and generously as though I deserved their help—because of them and because of the Library of Congress itself which remains, despite the vicissitudes of its history, one of the great glories of the Republic.

ARCHIBALD MACLEISH

Conway, Massachusetts
September 1970

Acknowledgments

Many of the selections included in this book appeared in *A Time to Speak, A Time to Act*, and *A Continuing Journey*, by Archibald MacLeish, published by Houghton Mifflin Company, and are used with the author's and publisher's permission, which is gratefully acknowledged. I also wish to express appreciation to the following periodicals among whose pages the following selections first appeared: *ALA Bulletin* for "Toward an Intellectual Offensive," "The Librarian and the Democratic Process," "The Library of Congress Protects Its Collections," and "A Tower Which Will Not Yield." *American Review on the Soviet Union* for "A Slavic Center for the Library of Congress." *Atlantic Monthly* for "Of the Librarian's Profession." *Bulletin of the Pan American Union* for "The American Experience." *DC Libraries* for "The Obligation of Libraries in a Democracy." *Library Journal* for "Changes in the Ritual of Library Dedication" and "Libraries in the Contemporary Crisis." *Library Quarterly* for "The Reorganization of the Library of Congress, 1939–44." *Massachusetts Library Association Bulletin* for "The Library of Congress and National Defense." *Personnel Administration* for "Library of Congress Employee Relations." *Publishers' Weekly* for "The Strongest and the Most Enduring Weapons." *Times* (London) for "The Intellectual Needs of Liberated Peoples."

Thanks are due also to the University of Chicago Press for permission to reprint "The Library and the Nation," which was first published in *Books and Libraries in Wartime* (University of Chicago Press, 1945, pages 141–54), Pierce Butler, editor.

Miss Pauline Cianciolo, of the American Library Association, deserves my particular gratitude for suggesting that I undertake this project and for help and guidance in its early stages. To her colleagues, particularly Mr. Richard A. Gray and Miss Marion Dittman, I wish to express my appreciation for their generous assistance in the editing and production of the book.

Most especially do I wish to acknowledge my debt to Mr. MacLeish, without whose support and cooperation this anthology of his writings on librarianship would not have been possible. Despite his preoccupation with his current creative activities, he generously gave of his time to answer my numerous questions and to lend his advice when I sought it. At my request, he edited the hitherto unpublished address which now bears the title "Libraries and Mass Communication." He also contributed the delightfully personal Preface which introduces the present work. For all of this, I am profoundly grateful.

EVA M. GOLDSCHMIDT

Introduction

Archibald MacLeish's career as librarian was brief, and his renown as writer and poet, to say nothing of his other varied achievements, has overshadowed his important contribution to librarianship. What is more, those librarians who are aware of the fact that he served as Librarian of Congress from 1939 to 1944 are more likely to remember the unfortunate controversy surrounding his appointment than the successful administrator and brilliant spokesman for the profession he turned out to be.

To put the story in perspective, one must go back a little in the history of the Library of Congress. From Civil War days to 1939 the Library had been, except for a short interval, under the direction of two men, Ainsworth Rand Spofford and Herbert Putnam. Under Putnam's leadership (from 1899 to 1939) the Library had increased its holdings from about a million to about six million volumes of books and pamphlets, not counting maps, newspapers, music, prints, and manuscripts running into the millions. The Library of Congress classification scheme was devised, cataloging practices became standardized, the printed card service was inaugurated, the Union Catalog had its beginnings, and in 1930 Congress authorized the construction of the Annex just across the street from the original building which had been completed in 1897.[1] Thus, to use MacLeish's words, "The Library of Congress in 1939 was not so much

1

an organization in its own right as the lengthened shadow of a man."[2] No wonder that the question of the succession to the office of Librarian of Congress aroused unusual interest.

Already toward the end of 1937 Herbert Putnam had indicated a desire to retire. The Executive Board of the American Library Association promptly appointed a committee to advise President Roosevelt on the nomination of a successor.[3] Throughout 1938 and the spring of 1939 the committee sought in vain to obtain an interview with the President. As time elapsed and no nomination was forthcoming, the ALA intensified its campaign, and at the instigation of the Association's officers letters from librarians started to arrive in large numbers at the White House and congressional offices.[4]

Meanwhile, the man who spurned this well-intentioned advice confessed to his friend, Justice Felix Frankfurter, that he had "had a bad time picking a librarian to succeed Putnam." He had, he said, "been tempted to appoint Archibald MacLeish" and wondered what Frankfurter thought. Admittedly, MacLeish was not a librarian, "nor a special student of incunabula or ancient manuscripts." Nevertheless, Roosevelt thought, "he has lots of qualifications that said specialists have not."[5] In reply Frankfurter not only warmly endorsed MacLeish's candidacy, but he also tried, apparently successfully, to allay Roosevelt's misgivings regarding MacLeish's lack of professional training. "What is wanted in the directing head of a great library," Frankfurter wrote, is "imaginative energy and vision." He should be "a man who knows books, loves books, and makes books. If he has these three qualities, the craftsmanship of the library calling is an easily acquired quality."[6]

On 6 June 1939, President Roosevelt made known his nomination of MacLeish to be Librarian of Congress.[7] An immediate furore arose, both in Congress and among professional librarians. Violent anti-New Dealers saw in the appointment of this alleged pro-Communist and fellow traveler one more bit of evidence of "Communist influence on appointments emanating from the White House."[8] Librarians were outraged at the nomination of a nonprofessional. The incumbent President of the American Library Association indignantly told the press that to appoint MacLeish as Librarian of Congress was about the same "as appointing a man Secretary of Agriculture, because he likes cut flowers on his dinner table."[9]

The general burden of the argument against MacLeish's appointment was that "there is a great deal more to being Librarian of Congress than possession of an ignorance of the Dewey Decimal system,"[10] and that in appointing an "untrained and unqualified person" the President was coming "to the aid of the enemy," just as the American Library Association was "beginning to win its nationwide battle" for recognition of librarianship as an established profession.[11] "Politicians, university authorities, and other appointers" would "not be slow in taking the President's cue." More library positions were likely to be filled from outside the profession,[12] which would thus be "less attractive to ambitious and able recruits."[13] A nonprofessional could not truly represent the Library of Congress, which was "in a special sense . . . the representative and symbol of the whole body of American librarians," unless MacLeish's selection implied that "the claim that librarianship is a profession is all bunkum."[14]

Although the American Library Association claimed that in its opposition to MacLeish's appointment it spoke for 90 percent of American librarians,[15] the nomination was warmly defended by some leading librarians and nonlibrarians alike. The *New York Times* editorially endorsed the appointment.

The Staff Association of the New York Public Library urged prompt senatorial confirmation.[16] Writing editorially in the *Saturday Review of Literature*, Henry Seidel Canby dismissed the charges of MacLeish's pro-Communist sympathies as "that familiar red herring." The real issue, as he saw it, was whether the head of a great library should be a specialist "in the technique of bookgetting and bookkeeping, or should be an executive broadly trained who has demonstrated his scholarship, his ability to organize, and his capacity for representing a great storehouse of intellectual energy."[17]

Other supporters of MacLeish unanimously cited his successful career as lawyer, poet, writer, editor of *Fortune* magazine, and curator of the Niemann Collection of Journalism at Harvard University. Although a poet, they said, he was not a dreamer.[18] "Far from moongazing," he was "a thoroughly practical workman of marked executive ability and extraordinary energy." Efficient and sensitive, he had the ability to inspire affection and confidence in all who worked with him.[19] He was a man of vision and a humanitarian.[20] Librarians should welcome a man of MacLeish's character and talents and not set up requirements so stringent that an able scholar and administrator could not readily join their ranks.[21]

The campaign against MacLeish's confirmation shifted into high gear when the ALA membership gathered in San Francisco for its 61st annual conference June 18-24, 1939. The Executive Board, on June 18, sent a protest letter to President Roosevelt and members of the Senate, asserting that confirmation of MacLeish would be "a calamity," because he "lacked the essential qualifications of a librarian." Library services "would almost certainly deteriorate under amateur leadership." Two members delegated to represent the Association at the hearing of the Senate Library Committee on 21 June 1938 soon reported back, however, that the matter seemed practically settled and that their strenuous protestations appeared to be of no avail. Indeed, the committee voted unanimously to recommend confirmation.[22]

This was the signal for further frantic activity by the ALA leadership, but thanks to Ralph Munn, president-elect of the Association, saner counsels prevailed in the end. Speaking at the closing session of the conference, Mr. Munn made it clear that he would do nothing further to oppose MacLeish's confirmation. On the contrary, he would ask the Executive Board for authority to write to MacLeish (in the event of his confirmation), explaining that opposition had not been based on personal feeling but solely on the ground of lack of training and that—having fought and lost—the Association would not "sulk like spoiled children."[23] When the Senate confirmed MacLeish's appointment on June 29 by a vote of sixty-four to eight,[24] Mr. Munn kept his word and offered the new librarian the Association's "complete and most friendly cooperation." MacLeish promptly and graciously accepted the proffered olive branch.[25]

The task which the poet-turned-librarian assumed officially on Monday, 2 October 1939, was staggering. An incredibly cumbersome and diffuse administrative structure, huge backlogs in every department of processing, delays in acquisitions, the uneven quality of the collections in the absence of a well-defined acquisitions policy, reference services scattered unsystematically among the Library's numerous departments and divisions—these were but some of the problems awaiting solution. MacLeish set to work immediately to deal with the most pressing needs and to revamp the organizational pattern. In the words of one of his colleagues:

The staff sensed at once that the new chief possessed unusual personal qualities, a first-rate mind, which absorbed and penetrated and understood; energies that could be at once exhausting, graceful and yet dynamic; marked powers of concentration and concern for rationalization; an insistence on definition; and a gift of expression beyond any similar gift they had ever known. And the staff was aware also of abilities as an administrator. But he was (and is) a poet, and it was not always possible to know at once in which capacity he confronted his subordinates. His drive was tremendous, and the fresh air that he brought with him was invigorating. Working with Archibald MacLeish was almost never easy, but it was almost always fun. His spirit of mission was contagious; he gave libraries (and particularly his own Library) a consciousness of new duties and new responsibilities.[26]

Not only the staff of the Library of Congress but the profession as a whole responded warmly to MacLeish's vigorous leadership. In contrast to the acrimonious debate at the 1939 ALA meeting, another conference of the Association, this time at Milwaukee, on 26 June 1942, gave him a "thunderous and spontaneous personal ovation," and "he was introduced by another President as the best friend of American libraries."[27]

As chief executive of a venerable institution badly in need of modernization, MacLeish has left an impressive record. He introduced modern fiscal and administrative concepts, arranged for systematic surveys of the collections, defined goals and priorities for acquisitions and services, and initiated progressive personnel policies. As his successor, Dr. Luther Evans, put it:

The outstanding characteristic of that brilliant episode is not the fact that so much was consummated in so short a time, but rather that there is now so little to repent.[28]

Another leading librarian wrote that it was the considered judgment of librarians who knew Mac-Leish best and who had seen him in action that it is doubtful that anyone else could have accomplished as much as he did in five years.[29] It is surprising, therefore, that the only account of the reorganization of the Library was written by MacLeish himself in 1944 for the *Library Quarterly* (October 1944). It gives a clear and detailed picture of MacLeish's actions as they evolved step by step and of his underlying approach and philosophy. It should be required reading for every library administrator seeking a rational, functional basis for his operations and an antidote to institutional inertia with all its attendant problems of antiquated collections, disintegrating services, communications breakdowns, low staff morale, and the like.

The excerpts from the official reports rendered by MacLeish as Librarian of Congress are included in this collection not merely to demonstrate that even government documents can make good reading, but to underscore MacLeish's dynamic approach to every aspect of library administration.

Time has invalidated neither MacLeish's specific measures nor his analyses of the issues perennially confronting library executives. The results he achieved during his five-year stint in Washington are the more remarkable if we keep in mind that he operated under wartime strains and stresses and also served as head of the Office of Facts and Figures and as Assistant Director of the Office of War Information during part of that time. His two short articles dealing with protection of the library's collections and the special services the library was called upon to perform for defense agencies give a bare hint of the magnitude and complexity of the problems created by global hostilities.

The primary reason for the publication of the present volume, however, derives from another aspect of MacLeish's efforts. There have been capable administrators and innovators before and since. MacLeish's unique and lasting contribution lies in the fact that he supplied the perspectives needed to make library activity meaningful in a society beset by a multitude of problems.

In the exquisite idiom of the poet he defined the role he believed librarians must play in a time when the nation's democratic heritage was threatened by aggression abroad and obscurantism at home. Fascism was the immediate danger against which MacLeish spoke out. But his insistence that librarians cannot be "neutral, passive, negative," that their profession "must become instead the affirmative and advocating profession of the attorney for a cause," applies with equal force to the contemporary scene.[30] In fact, he charged librarians with a degree of social responsibility which they have only very recently and very haltingly begun to accept.

MacLeish saw in the education of "all the people of this country . . . to the value of the democratic tradition they have inherited" the chief weapon against the alienation, ignorance, prejudice, and superstition which breed fascism and other forms of extremism. By necessity, he believed, the burden of this education must be entrusted to libraries, because "libraries alone are staffed by people whose disinterestedness is beyond suspicion." They alone "are capable of acting directly upon the present adult generation." It was not enough, he insisted, for librarians "to secure books intelligently and to make them readily available to inquirers." They must learn how to get readers for their books.[31] They must "make use of every means at their disposal to bring to the people of this country a disinterested, informed account of the means of education at their disposition."[32] He envisioned librarianship as a sort of "legislative reference service" serving "not Congress only or a legislature, but a people."

By accepting the challenge that the nature of the times presented, librarians might not only serve the cause of civilization. In the process, the profession—unable in the past "to arrive at a common agreement as to the social end which librarianship exists to serve"—might find "the definition of its function for which it has sought so long." By fulfilling the responsibilities incumbent upon them in a democratic society at war, librarians might, in other words, achieve an intelligent consensus as to what librarianship is essentially all about.

Have we, as librarians, met the challenge of the forties? Are we, as librarians, meeting the challenges of the sixties and seventies? Or do we still have a long way to go before we will "become active and not passive agents of the democratic process"?[33] What account have we given of ourselves in the "battle to maintain the power and authority of truth and free intelligence"? Do we "sit back in a humble and defensive silence," awaiting the onslaught of those who seek to destroy "the city of learning"? Do we belong to those who "have not perceived that the defense of the country of the mind involves an affirmation, an assertion of a fighting and affirmative belief in intellectual things"?[34]

Have we come to grips with the elusive problem of our professional role and image? Have we defined to our satisfaction the "inward function of librarianship," or are we still preoccupied with the "outward furniture of professionalism"?[35] Have the lessons of war been forgotten, or have we succeeded in convincing our contemporaries that libraries are "a vital necessity to a *nation*," rather than expendable "cultural luxuries,"[36] the pawns of politicians everywhere?

If we answer all these questions honestly, we will

be able to gauge the extent to which our performance has fallen short of the ideals held up before us by MacLeish a generation ago.

The dynamic role MacLeish sought for librarians in an age when the very foundations of human freedom and civilization were imperiled is predicated on the intellectual aspect of librarianship, which he emphasized with wit and wisdom. The distinction he makes between the book as a "physical object made of certain physical materials in a physical shape" and the "intellectual object made of all materials or of no materials and standing in as many shapes as there are forms and balances and structures in men's minds" gives to the librarian's work a dimension indispensable if we want to be true professionals, not mere technicians, "sort of check boys in the parcel room of culture."[37] Anyone following current library literature may be forgiven, however, for wondering whether this intellectual dimension has not been engulfed by a ceaseless stream of technical minutiae and pedestrian concerns. Only recently, it appears, has there been a growing awareness that a sound balance between scholarship and custodial chores is needed if librarianship is not to be an exercise in intellectual futility.

We librarians would do well, moreover, to search our souls to find whether we truly are as stout believers in the power of books as are those who burn them, because they fear their influence. As well we know, book burning and book banning did not go out of fashion with the defeat of nazism. Are we firmly convinced that "books were never more important to this country than they are today," that "books will play a tremendously important, a deeply serious role in the shaping of our history"?[38] Has our faith been undermined by the insidious urgings of those who see in nonprint media, in electronic hardware, in computerized stores of information, the wave of the future? Or do we believe with MacLeish that the ever growing spread of mass communication makes "the reading of books . . . important as it has never been before"? Do our activities reflect the conviction that libraries have become "the one means by which a vivid, different, living life may still be available to all men"? What are we doing to reach out to meet the needs of those who rebel against the "sameness and suffocation"[39] of our mass society, so that libraries will become bulwarks of individualism and human dignity?

MacLeish's response to the repression of political dissent resulting from the fears and suspicions generated by the cold war—a repression symbolized by the name of the late Senator Joseph McCarthy—was an impassioned plea for intellectual freedom delivered at the dedication of the Carleton College Library in 1956. He heaped scorn on those who sought "to withhold books, to suppress books, to censor books, to deny the people of a town or of a state or of the country the right to read books as they choose to read them." "It is the nerve center, the heart, of democracy," he warned, "which is struck at by these practices and measures, for the heart of democracy is the right of a people to make up their minds for themselves." No neutrality, he insisted, is possible on the issue of human freedom. "You cannot be neutral on that issue anywhere in the world we live in and least of all can you be neutral on it in a library." In the never ending struggle for freedom of the mind, "libraries must be strong points of defense."

Indeed, the struggle has by no means ceased. "Theoretically we all of us believe in the freedom of the mind." It remains for us to translate our theoretical belief into concrete, effective action to assist and protect "the unknown and unsung librarians who, with little backing from their fellow citizens, and with less economic security than would encourage most of the rest of us to be brave, have held an exposed and vulnerable front."[40]

Outwardly less dramatic but, in fact, more perplexing are the issues confronting librarians as a result of the "immeasurable rapidity with which the flood of scientific discovery has inundated our age." What has been the effect of the growing specialization, "the burgeoning babel, the increasing fragmentation" on human knowledge itself and "on the techniques for making that knowledge available, making it known at the time and place where it is needed"? In the answer to that question lies the future of the librarian's profession. In an age where the "ordinary educated man" is excluded from the "specialists' country," can the librarian at least place the "untranslatable knowledge" of the scientist in its spectrum? Can he give to his materials the "intellectual coherence" which distinguishes a library collection "from a warehouse full of printed pages"?

For the answer to these questions MacLeish does not look to the "miraculous electronic contraptions" of which we librarians hear so much and generally know so little. He cuts through the mystique of computer technology, which attributes to machines an independent logical capacity, by reminding us wryly that "even a computer must be programmed first." He neither underestimates nor rejects the capability for the storage and dissemination of facts which "information scientists" have developed. What we should not forget, however, is that "the great human need" is not for more and more information. On the contrary, "vast floods of unassimilated, uncomprehended knowledge" have been the bane of modern man. To resolve his existential dilemma he must turn to "books of poetry, books of high literature, books which hold the long and anxious record of man's unceasing search for knowledge of himself, his life, his death." "The man," in other words, "comes first before the information."[41]

I have chosen to arrange the pieces in this anthology chronologically. Although each piece in its own way is timeless, it does at the same time reflect the urgent concerns of its era: the dangers of Fascist aggression, the effects of global war, postwar reconstruction, the McCarthy witchhunts of the fifties, the "publication explosion" and the spread of automation in the sixties. Hence, this arrangement provides a natural continuity for those who wish to follow the progression of MacLeish's thought, without curbing others' inclination to skip and browse. But whether the selections here offered are perused singly or as a whole, each reading and rereading should prove increasingly rewarding. Events, names, people, places, have changed and will go on changing. The perspectives projected by MacLeish's brilliant prose, however, will continue to give to American librarianship a focus and direction without which it cannot play its proper part in bringing about the just and peaceful society we all hope for.

Notes

[1]Lucy Salamanca, *Fortress of Freedom* (Philadelphia: Lippincott, 1942), p.195-313.

[2]Archibald MacLeish, "The Reorganization of the Library of Congress."

[3]"MacLeish Appointment Protested," *ALA Bulletin* 33:467 (July 1939).

[4]"Librarianship of Congress," Proceedings of the 61st Annual Conference of the American Library Association, 18-24 June 1939, *ALA Bulletin* 33: P-55-56 (15 October 1939); "MacLeish Nomination Raises Controversy," *Publishers' Weekly* 135:2159-60 (17 June 1939).

[5]Letter from Franklin D. Roosevelt to Justice Felix Frankfurter, 3 May 1939, reprinted in David C. Mearns, "The Brush of the Comet: Archibald MacLeish at the Library of Congress," *Atlantic Monthly* 215:90 (May 1965).

⁶Letter from Felix Frankfurter to Franklin D. Roosevelt, 11 May 1939, reprinted in Mearns, op. cit.

⁷"Poet Named Librarian of Congress," *Library Journal* 64:508 (15 June 1939); "Archibald MacLeish Nominated Librarian of Congress," *Publishers' Weekly* 135:2116 (10 June 1939).

⁸"Panned Poet," *Newsweek* 13:18 (19 June 1939).

⁹"Library, Librarian," *Time* 33:18 (19 June 1939).

¹⁰Viola Mauseth, "MacLeish Appointment," *Saturday Review of Literature* 20:9 (1 July 1939).

¹¹Pelham Barr, "Letter to the Editor," *Publishers' Weekly* 135: 2119 (24 June 1939).

¹²"Forgetting the Library of Congress," *Book Life* 1:3–4 (October 1939).

¹³Arundell Esdale, "Librarian of Congress," *Library Association Record* 41:430 (August 1939).

¹⁴L. Stanley Jast, "Library and the Community," ibid., p.431.

¹⁵"Librarianship of Congress," *ALA Bulletin* 33:P-49 (15 October 1939).

¹⁶"MacLeish Nomination Raises Controversy," *Publishers' Weekly* 135:2159–60 (17 June 1939).

¹⁷Editorial, *Saturday Review of Literature* 20:8 (17 June 1939).

¹⁸John Chamberlain, "Archibald MacLeish," *Saturday Review of Literature* 20:10–11 (24 June 1939).

¹⁹"Librarianship of Congress," *ALA Bulletin* 33:P-50 (15 October 1939).

²⁰John T. Vance, "Discussion on MacLeish at the 34th Annual Meeting of American Association of Law Libraries," *Law Library Journal* 32:338–39 (September 1939).

²¹"Archibald MacLeish," *Wilson Library Bulletin* 14:57 (September 1939); Clarence S. Paine, "Looking Forward," ibid., p.138 (October 1939); L. M. Raney, "The MacLeish Case," *Library Journal* 64:522 (July 1939).

²²"Senate Confirms Appointment," *Publishers' Weekly* 136:102 (8 July 1939).

²³"Librarianship of Congress," *ALA Bulletin* 33: P-47–48, P-49–51, P-55–58, P-62–63 (15 October 1939).

²⁴"New Librarian of Congress," *Library Journal* 64:546 (July 1939).

²⁵Ralph Munn and Archibald MacLeish, "Let Us All Cooperate," ibid., p.570 (August 1939).

²⁶David C. Mearns, "The Story Up to Now," *Annual Report of the Librarian of Congress for the Fiscal Year Ending June 30, 1946* (Washington, D.C.: U.S. Govt. Print. Off., 1947), p.221.

²⁷Ibid., p.220.

[28]*Annual Report of the Librarian of Congress for the Fiscal Year Ending June 30, 1945* (Washington, D.C.: U.S. Govt. Print. Off., 1946), p.13.

[29]Keyes D. Metcalf, "Editorial Forum," *Library Journal* 70:213 (1 March 1945).

[30]"Of the Librarian's Profession."

[31]"Libraries in the Contemporary Crisis."

[32]"The Obligation of Libraries in a Democracy."

[33]"The Librarian and the Democratic Process."

[34]"Toward an Intellectual Offensive."

[35]"The Librarian and the Democratic Process."

[36]"The Library and the Nation."

[37]"Of the Librarian's Profession."

[38]"The Strongest and the Most Enduring Weapons."

[39]"Libraries and Mass Communication."

[40]"A Tower Which Will Not Yield."

[41]"Changes in the Ritual of Library Dedication."

Champion
of a cause

Libraries
in the contemporary
crisis · 1939

I have known for some months that
I was going to have the honor of speaking
to you this evening. But it was not until five days
ago that I learned what I was expected to say. Five
days ago I was sitting more or less comfortably at a
luncheon table in an Annapolis hotel, with my attention wholly given to the ice cream, when the learned
and distinguished gentleman on my left informed
me that the new Librarian of Congress was on the
point of rising and delivering a speech. When I
asked him what the new Librarian of Congress was
on the point of rising and delivering a speech about
he said, "That's easy. There is only one thing these
people want to know about you. They want to know
why on earth you did it."

It is an interesting question. Or rather, it is two
interesting questions. The first is a question interesting to that minority — an excessively small minority
if the sales of my books are correctly reported —
which likes to read my verse. To these rare people —
rare in every sense of the term — the question means
"Why on earth did you take a job as librarian which
will leave you little or no time for your own work?"
The second question is a question interesting apparently to a very much larger number of my fellow cit-

Founder's Day address at Carnegie Institute, Pittsburgh, Pa.,
19 October 1939. Reprinted from *Library Journal* 64:879–82 (15
November 1939), copyright © 1939 by R. R. Bowker Co.

izens, but interesting in a somewhat different way. When the *New York Herald Tribune* asked the new Librarian of Congress why on earth he did it, the *New York Herald Tribune* was not concerned for the unwritten verse of A. MacLeish. The question as the *Herald Tribune* asked it meant, "Why on earth did you take a job for which you are so patently unfitted."

But interesting though the question is I doubt if I shall attempt to answer it. There are two persuasive reasons. As asked by the *Herald Tribune* the question is not answerable—and is not meant to be. As asked by the readers of my books, it is answerable only at the cost of a personal history which you would find both long and dull.

There is however a question under this question, or within this question, or behind this question, which I should like to try to answer. It is a question addressed not to me, but to all men of responsibility. And it is a question which concerns not a particular librarian, but the librarians of the nation.

If you object that I have been a librarian for two weeks only and that I know nothing about libraries and that I should therefore not attempt to talk about libraries, I can only reply that the first statement is true, and that the second statement is true, but that the third statement is not true. For some months the librarians of the country have been talking quite freely about me without knowing anything about me. It is only fair that I should reciprocate.

Moreover, ignorance has never stopped the mouths of lecturers. On the contrary, American notions of American poetry are almost wholly formed by people who, if they spoke only out of knowledge, would not speak at all. For one Louis Untermyer who will patiently present to his audiences the important poetry of our generation in this country—the poetry of Pound and Eliot and Sandburg and Frost and Cummings and Crane—there are a hundred en-

lighteners of the people who not only do not understand the greater part of the work of these poets but
are not even certain, of their own knowledge, that it
exists.

There is no doubt that I am ignorant of American
libraries. American writers generally are unaware of
American libraries except as imposing frontages on
important streets. . . . and the fault, I may add, is
not altogether with the writers. But ignorant though
I am I have several precedents for speech. And I
have also a compelling reason—the reason more
compelling than any other—the reason of time.

Our age, as many men have noticed, is an age
characterized by the tyranny of time. Never more
than at this moment was that tyranny evident.
Those of us who are concerned, for whatever reason,
with the preservation of the civilization and the inherited culture of this nation find ourselves in a situation in which time is running out, not like the sand
in a glass, but like the blood in an opened artery.
There is still time left to us. But we can foresee
clearly the moment when there will be none.

I do not like epigrammatic condensations of history. I do not like analyses of life which present its situations on the brutal balance of an "either" and an
"or." But it seems to me no less than exact to say
that the situation which now confronts us in this
country is a situation which must be expressed in
just these terms.

We face a situation which has an "either" and
which has an "or" and we will choose or fail to
choose between them. Whichever we do we will
have chosen. For the failure to choose in the world
we live in is in itself a choice. The "either" as I see it
is the education of the people of this country. The
"or" is fascism. We will either educate the people of
this republic to know and therefore to value and
therefore to preserve their own democratic culture

or we will watch the people of this republic trade their democratic culture for the nonculture, the obscurantism, the superstition, the brutality, the tyranny which is overrunning eastern and central and southern Europe.

Others, I will admit, see the alternatives in different terms. Six and seven years ago at the bottom of the depression American intellectuals saw the American progress as a race between economic reform and violent revolution. Economics, as you will recall, was then the one, the true religion which explained everything. If you made the economic machine operate you made everything operate: if you didn't make the economic machine operate everything collapsed. The "either" in those days was economic salvation: the "or" was social ruin. That, however, was before Herr Hitler had demonstrated that men could be led against their economic interests as well as against their spiritual interests if the propaganda was good enough.

Another, and a still popular definition of the American alternatives was, and is, the definition which puts Americanism on one side and a Conspiracy of Evil on the other. The nature of the conspiracy depends on the angle of observation. To certain good Americans the conspirators are the Communists. There was, and there still is, some disagreement as to what a Communist is (and some of the disagreement is honest) but there is no disagreement as to the general theory. The theory is that America is all right and the Americans are all right and everything else would be all right, if only the Communists could be prevented from spreading their insidious propaganda and wrecking the country. It is not, I think you will agree, a very flattering picture of America despite the fact that it is a picture offered by those who are loudest in their protestations of love for the country. It implies that the Americanism of the rest of the Americans is so shaky and insecure, and the appeal to them of Communist dogma is so seductive that only by stopping American ears with legal wax and strapping American arms with legal thongs can American democracy be preserved. I for one have never been impressed by the sincerity of those whose eagerness to save American democracy is so great that they would gladly destroy all the American guarantees of freedom to ask, freedom to answer, freedom to think, and freedom to speak, which make American democracy democratic. I more than half suspect that it is not America but some other institution, something very different, something very much smaller, very much less admirable, these people really wish to save.

But the self-appointed guardians of America have not been the only ones to see the American situation as a conspiracy of the forces of evil. The people they hate most, the Communists themselves, take exactly the same position. They take it, however, with this difference—that the conspiracy as the Communists see it is a conspiracy of evil persons from the other end of the political rainbow. The Communist conspirators are conspirators who meet in bankers' dens furnished with black leather armchairs and boxes of Havana stogies to plot the ruin of the people.

The shallowness and romanticism of both these pictures of the contemporary crisis are obvious. No one of twelve-year intelligence who really thinks about it believes for one moment that American democracy is endangered by conspiracies—least of all by conspiracies like these. If there is any danger in this direction it is the danger introduced by those who talk about these alleged conspiracies; not by those who theoretically take part. For the only effect of such romantic talk is to distract the attention of the citizens from the actual situation. Those who shout that America is threatened by the reds prevent a certain number of their fellow citizens from considering soberly and quietly what it is that really threatens America. And those, on the other side, who attribute all our dangers to a Wall Street conspiracy to corrupt the army and take over the government, divert the minds of their listeners from the much less romantic but much more disturbing truth.

For the truth is that the threat to free culture and democratic civilization in the United States is the threat not of any person and not of any group of persons but of a condition. Those who, like myself, assert that the threat to a free culture and a democratic civilization in this country is the threat of fascism, do not mean by that word what the Communist Party meant by it — or pretended to mean by it — before the Russo-German Pact. Those who, like myself, assert that the threat to democratic civilization in this country is the threat of fascism mean that the culture of the Republic is threatened by the existence in the United States of the kind of situation which has produced fascism elsewhere, and that that situation in the United States has already given indications, human and other, of developing in the known direction. In the same way those who say that the alternative to fascism is education do not mean that democracy can be saved by educating the people to see conspirators under the bed, but that democracy can be saved by educating the people to value the kind of life democracy makes possible.

The situation which has produced fascism elsewhere and which threatens to produce fascism here is a situation with which education can deal because it is a situation which failure of education has created. The situation which produced fascism in Germany and in Italy, and which threatens to produce fascism here, is a situation the historical background of which is clear enough. The industrial revolution, with its need for specialized labor, created a new economic class, the so-called lower middle class, above and distinct from the masses of the people who labor with their hands. The capitalist money system, with its tendency to squeeze society into pyramidal forms, froze this new-made class into the social order. The result was to suspend a great mass of people in a kind of limbo just above brute labor, just below comfort and decency and self-respect. Freed on the one side from the discipline of labor by the hand, they were excluded on the other from the discipline of labor by the head. Deprived on the one side of the realism, the hard-headedness, the piety, the traditional human wisdom, the salt sense, the kindness of those who labor the earth and the earth's metals with their bodies, they were equally deprived on the other of that different kindness, that different knowledge, that different wisdom of those whose life is in the mind.

They were, in other words, a class for which the old education of habit and custom had been broken and for which a new education of intelligence and reason had not been supplied. Fascism is the image of that fact. When this class, driven to revolt by the failures of the economic system which had created it, put forward its leaders — its Mussolinis and its Hitlers — it conducted itself precisely as a class so deserted by the culture of its society might be expected to conduct itself. The reason why fascism is so brutal, so vulgar, so envious, so superstitious, so childish, so shrewd, is that these are the characteristics of a social class excluded from the moral and emotional and intellectual traditions of its society. The reason why fascism makes flags and parades its symbols is that no other symbols are moving to those who have not been allowed to inherit the culture of their past. The reason why fascism makes war and hate its aim is that those out of whose misery fascism is created, are men incapable of imagining any other ends except the ends of hate and war.

But the fact, the evident fact, the fact which must at all times be held in view in the United States is the fact that fascism is the image of a condition, not the invention of a man, and that the condition which has created fascism in Europe may very easily create fascism here UNLESS we act and act now to prevent it. And the question—the always asking question—the question which history presents to us and will continue to present to us no matter how we close our eyes or turn our minds away, is the question HOW we shall act? Shall we turn our attention to the war in Europe and do what we can to encourage those who are fighting fascism there? Shall we organize patriotic displays at home and punish those who preach fascism directly or indirectly here? Or shall we as honestly as we can, as directly as we can, and as effectively as we can, attempt to change by education the condition from which fascism results?

To my mind there is no doubt as to the answer we should give. I am aware, I think, of some at least of the difficulties. I am aware that the immediate forces which drive the intellectually and culturally dispossessed into fascism are economic forces and that education is not an altogether adequate answer to those who ask for a chance to work usefully and creatively and to fulfill their lives. I am aware also that there are people in the United States who do not wish to admit that there are large numbers of their fellow citizens who have been excluded from the American tradition and the American culture. But I think, notwithstanding these difficulties and objections and many others, that we have no choice but to make use of the one effective weapon we know ourselves to possess. If we respect prejudice because it calls itself patriotism we are poor patriots. If we wait for the economic restoration of a world at war we will wait too long. As things are, in the world as it is, we can either attempt to educate the people of this country — ALL the people of this country — to the value of the democratic tradition they have inherited, and so admit them to its enjoyment, or we can watch some of the people of this country destroy that tradition for the rest.

It is this issue, as I see it, which is presented to American libraries, for it is upon American libraries that the burden of this education must fall. It cannot fall upon the schools. There is no longer time to await the education of a new generation which will come in due course to a more enlightened maturity. It cannot be left to the newspapers or the magazines however earnest their protestations of honesty and disinterestedness. There are honest publishers, but there are no disinterested publishers and there never will be. It cannot, even more obviously, be left to the moving pictures or the radio. The radio's notion of disinterestedness is equal time to both sides regardless of the sides; the moving picture's notion of disinterestedness is silence. But this burden CAN be entrusted to the libraries. The libraries and the libraries alone can carry it. The libraries alone are capable of acting directly upon the present adult generation. The libraries alone are staffed by people whose disinterestedness is beyond suspicion. And though there are occasional directors of libraries and boards of library trustees who will stoop to the exclusion of books which offend their social or political or economic preconceptions — books, let us say, like *The Grapes of Wrath* — the directors and trustees of libraries are in general men with the highest sense of their duties to their institutions and their country. The libraries, in brief, are the only institutions in the United States capable of dealing with the contemporary crisis in American life in terms and under conditions which give promise of success. They are the only institutions in American life capable of opening to the citizens of the Republic a knowledge of the wealth and richness of the culture which a century and a half of democratic life has produced.

That fact is a fact which should properly fill the librarians of this country with a sense of pride. But it is a fact also which should fill them with a sense of responsibility. For at the present moment, as librarians themselves have been the first to admit, they are not opening that knowledge and that understanding to the citizens of the Republic. The American Library Association has this year published a small but most important, as well as most readable, study of American librarianship by Wilhelm Munthe, Director of the University Library at Oslo, in which the achievements of American libraries in this direction are analyzed. According to such studies and surveys as he found available, Dr. Munthe concludes that in "an ordinary good library town" the library card holders comprise some 25 to 30 per cent of the population; that half of these are school children; that of the remaining adult card holders "a large portion never use their cards"; that of the remainder of that remainder 50 per cent are high school students, 21 per cent are housewives, 2½ per cent are business men, 5 per cent are clerks, 5 per cent are skilled labor and 5 per cent are unskilled labor. In other words clerks, business men, and laborers using the library in an "ordinary good library town" amount altogether to less than a fifth of an undetermined portion of 15 per cent of the population. This figure, says Dr. Munthe, "is amazingly low." One admires his restraint.

The truth seems to be that American libraries have executed magnificently the first half of their assignment, as that assignment was defined some fifty years ago by my distinguished predecessor in the Library of Congress. They have solved with great brilliance the problem of getting books for readers. They have developed practices of accession, cataloging, and classification, which enable them to secure books intelligently and to make them readily available to inquirers. But they have not executed the second half of their assignment. They have not learned how to get READERS for BOOKS. The typical American library borrower can still be described by a friendly but informed and intelligent European in Dr. Munthe's words:

> A woman, of twenty-three and one-half years, with three years of high school, who borrows in the course of a month four modern novels of no particular worth, one really good novel and one popular biography or entertaining travel account.

And who are her authors? As Dr. Munthe tells us:

> We can safely say that they are not the ones whose names will some day be cut in marble on the face of library buildings. The are people like Berta Ruck, Zane Grey and Kathleen Norris. . . . Authors with troublesome or radical ideas are definitely avoided.

If the learned Doctor is right the libraries of America have a tremendous distance to go before they can feel that they have found the readers their books deserve. But it is not a journey they must make alone. Behind them, far back but still livingly there, are the men who created the American library system—men like the man in whose memory this day is celebrated. Beside them are the many still alive—writers, teachers, lovers of American liberty—to whom the education of the people for the preservation of their culture is the best and most hopeful undertaking open to our time: the many who believe as I do that we can either educate the people of this

Republic to know and therefore to value and to preserve their own democratic culture, or we can watch
the people of this Republic trade their democratic
culture for the ignorance and the prejudice and the
hate of which the just and proper name is fascism.

These are the alternatives our time presents us.
They are not alternatives which will remain forever
open. We may accept them now or lose them now.
"History," says Wystan Auden,

> History to the defeated
> Can say Alas but cannot help or pardon.

History can say Alas to this American civilization
of ours as well as to any other. Unless we save it.
Unless we act, not only with our words but with our
MINDS, to save it.

The American experience
· 1939

This is an occasion without precedent in the history of the Library of Congress. But not perhaps for the reason of which you think. It is an occasion without precedent in the history of the Library of Congress because it is the first time in the Library's history when the Librarian has opened a new building or a new division with a speech.

The Library moved across from the Capitol to the building in which we stand to the accompaniment of an eloquent and admired silence. Forty years later it pushed its frontiers across the street to the Annex which can be seen from these windows without a single word. Today it opens its Hispanic Room with a speech by the Librarian.

Unkind critics or unkinder friends will suggest that the difference is a difference in Librarians — that my predecessor being truly a librarian knew the golden value of that silence to which students in libraries are continually admonished whereas I, being a versifier, suffer from the itch for words which has always characterized my calling. It is a plausible explanation for it contains much truth. There is indeed a difference in Librarians and a difference, I fear, for the worse.

Address delivered on the occasion of the dedication of the Hispanic Room in the Library of Congress, 12 October 1939. First published in the *Bulletin of the Pan American Union* 73:621–24 (November 1939).

But the real explanation is not this. The real explanation is that the times change as well as the men. There are times when a great institution can let stone and mortar speak for it. And there are other times when it must attempt to speak, however haltingly, for itself.

This is such a time. Once the value of the things of the spirit could be taken for granted. Once it could be taken for granted anywhere in the civilized world that the free inquiry of the free spirit was essential to the dignified and noble life of man. Once it could be assumed as a matter of course that the work of artists, the work of poets, the work of scholars, was good and should be respected, and would be preserved. Now it is no longer possible to assume these things. Now—and it is still incredible to us that it should be true—now such an act of faith in the life of the human spirit as we perform here today, such an act of respect for the labor of poets and scholars and of love for that which they have made, cannot be taken for granted: cannot be left to speak for itself even in a room as beautiful, as eloquent as this. It is necessary for us to say what it is that we are doing and why it is that we are doing it.

I for one am not proud of this necessity. I am not glad that it is necessary to speak.

What we do is this: we dedicate here a room and a division of the Library of Congress which has been set apart for the preservation and the study and the honor of the literature and scholarship of those other republics which share with ours the word American; and which share with ours also the memories of human hope and human courage which that word evokes—evokes now as never before in the history of our hemisphere.

Why we do it is also obvious. We do it because this literature and this scholarship are worthy in themselves of the closest study and the most meticulous care and the greatest veneration; and because they, more than any other literature and more than any other scholarship, help us in this republic to understand the American past which is common to us all.

We are beginning to perceive, as the peaceful dream of the Nineteenth Century fades away and the economic theories and scientific theories, which were to explain everything, fade away ·vith it—we are beginning to perceive that man never was, and never can be, such a philosophic abstraction as the thinkers of that century supposed—that man is a creature living on this earth and that the earth he lives on qualifies his life. America has shaped and qualified and redirected the lives of men living on her continents for four hundred years. But we who are born in America and live our lives here, have not very well understood our relations to these continents, nor our debt to them, nor in what way they have altered us and changed our bodies and our minds.

We have not understood this because we have turned, for the most part, to the literature and the scholarship of Europe for instruction, and for the interpretation of our world. Those of us who were of Latin origin have turned to the literatures of latinized Europe, and those of us who were of English and Celtic and Scandinavian and Teutonic origin to the literatures of northern Europe. We have found there great treasures, great wisdom, high instruction—but only rarely an interpretation of our own lives in terms of the earth we know. Even the American child reading his European poems feels the strangeness; the seasons are wrong, the springs too early or too slow, the birds and animals different.

It is a curious condition but one which, by long habit, we have come to take as natural. We have looked at America with borrowed European eyes so long that we should hardly recognize the country if we saw it with our own. Doubtless we shall continue for many generations to look at America with these eyes. Our cultural inheritance is European by origin, and like other European legatees of other legacies we can enjoy it only in the original currency. Which means inevitably that we employ that original currency to value our American lives. But though it is inevitable that the great richness of our European past should impose its values upon our American present, it is not inevitable, and it is surely not desirable, that the great richness of our European past should exclude us from the richness of our own.

From the beginning of the sixteenth century there has been accumulating on these continents a body of recorded American experience of the very greatest importance to anyone concerned to understand the American earth and the relation of that earth to the men who live upon it. Because this experience has been recorded in several languages and because it has been deposited in scattered places — places as far apart as Santiago de Chile and Bogotá and Buenos Aires and Mexico City and New Orleans and St. Louis and Quebec — because, furthermore, it has been overlaid with the continuing importation of European literature and European thought — for all these reasons the recorded American experience has not influenced the common life of the Americas as it should have influenced it. It has not been useful to an understanding of the Americas as it should have been useful.

Other men who know these continents better than I know them — other men who know these records of the American experience better than I shall ever know them — will think of many instances in their own lives when the words of men who lived in the Americas before them have made suddenly clear, and suddenly explicable, matters they had long wished to understand. But even in my shallow knowledge of these things there is one such indebtedness. Some twelve years ago in a Paris library I came upon a copy of Bernal Díaz' *True History of the Conquest of New Spain*. There in that still living, still human, still sharply breathing and believable story of Mexico it seemed to me that I understood for the first time the central American experience — the experience which is American because it can be nothing else — the experience of all those who, of whatever tongue, are truly American — the experience of the journey westward from the sea into the unknown and dangerous country beyond which lies the rich and lovely city for which men hope.

I tried at that time to make a poem of this understanding. The argument of my poem began —

Of that world's conquest and the fortunate wars:
Of the great report and expectation of honor:
How in their youth they stretched sail: how fared they
Westward under the wind: by wave wandered:
Shoaled ship at the last at the ends of ocean:
How they were marching in the lands beyond:
Of the difficult ways there were and the winter's snow:
Of the city they found in the good lands:
   how they lay in it:
How there was always the leaves and the days
   going . . .

Other men will say the same thing in other words and many of them better. Historians will tell us how their study of the documents and monuments of Mexico and Peru opened to their minds the true perspective of American civilization — a civilization of which the first European date is the year 1523 when a school for Indian boys was opened in Mexico City — of which the first American date lies deep under the limestone waters of Yucatán and the iron earth of Guatemala. Scholars will speak of the year 1539 when the first book to be printed in the Americas was printed in the city of Mexico. Lovers of human liberty will remember the name of Carlos de Sigüenza y Góngora who, in the year 1691, at a time when witches were being hung in Salem, successfully defended against the ecclesiastics of Mexico his opinion that the great eclipse of that year was a natural event. They will quote against all witch-burners in all centuries and countries his noble words: "I stood with my quadrant and telescope viewing the [blackened] sun, extremely happy and repeatedly thanking God for having granted that I might behold what so rarely happens in a given place and about which there are so few observations in the books."

No man living in the United States can truly say he knows the Americas unless he has a knowledge of these things — a knowledge of this other American past, this older American past which shares with ours the unforgettable experience of the journey toward the West and the westward hope.

What we are doing in this room, then, is to dedicate to the uses of the citizens of the United States, and to the uses of learners and readers everywhere, these records of the American experience. In this Hispanic Room of the Library, students of the Americas may follow the great Iberian tradition which has populated with its ideas and its poetry by far the greater part of these two continents. Here they may read the rich and various works written in these continents in the Iberian tongues — the two great tongues which, with our own, have become the American language. Here, if our hopes are realized, Americans may some day find the greatest collection of Hispanic literature and scholarship ever gathered in one place.

There are men in the world today — and many rather than few — who say that the proper study of mankind is not man but a particular kind of man. There are those who teach that the only cultural study proper to a great people is its own culture. There are those also who say that the only real brotherhood is that blood brotherhood for which so many wars have been fought and by which so many deaths are still justified. The dedication of this room and of this collection of books is a demonstration of the fact that these opinions are not valid in the Americas: that in the Americas, peopled by so many hopes, so many sufferings, so many races, the highest brotherhood is still the brotherhood of the human spirit and the true study is the study of the best.

This is the belief of the people of this Republic expressed by the action of their national Library in the dedication of this room.

The obligation
of libraries in a democracy
· 1940

There are numerous reasons why
laymen should not be appointed to administer professional establishments. Some of them
have been lately heard. They are eloquent and they
are weightily supported. But weighty though they
may be there is one small countervailing consideration which should perhaps be advanced. It can hardly
be advanced in the serious hope that it will rebut
the premise but it may be advanced notwithstanding.
It is the consideration that laymen, precisely because
they are laymen, are inclined to ask questions. Lay
Secretaries of the Navy have asked questions about
ships which first amused and then enraged and finally astonished professional sailors, and lay Secretaries of the Treasury have asked questions about
money which no banker in his senses would ever
think of asking because no banker in his senses
would reply.

I do not suggest that such questions are sensible
questions. I suggest merely that they are asked and
that the asking has a certain value. If no one but the
general public asked the learned professions what
they were up to and why they were up to it, the
learned professions would never bother to reply. And

Address delivered before the District of Columbia Library Association. First published in *DC Libraries* 11, no.2:17–18 (January
1940).

if the learned professions did not bother to reply the learned professions would shortly find themselves inhabiting those lamaseries of the intellect to which no travelers come. For all professional men, as all professional men know of their own experience, tend to make purposes of practices, and to build the habitual mechanism of a means into the final justification of an end.

I speak of this not philosophically or in abstract but with an immediate and present interest, for I find myself, as the lay administrator of a great library, filled with questions of a naïveté which astonishes even myself. I find myself asking not only why this particular thing is done in this particular way, but *what* it is the library *as* a library is doing. I find myself asking, in short, what a library is and what a library should do. What is a public library, a national library, in a great democracy? What are its obligations to the democratic government which established it?

Historically I think I know the answer. When democratic governments first admitted an obligation to maintain libraries for the people it was assumed that the obligation was fulfilled by the simple maintenance of adequate collections of books to which readers could have recourse if they wished. It was no concern of government if readers *neglected* to have recourse to the books. It was merely the misfortune and improvidence of the neglectful readers. Government at that time admitted no affirmative concern with the education of the citizens. Its concern ended with the schooling of the young. Beyond that, the only duty of a civilized government was to make the *means* of education available. Education at this level was known in the language of the time as self-improvement. It was a means of improving yourself—improving your mind and thus improving your chances of improving your salary. Government had no interest in it beyond the democratic and impersonal interest of making the means of self-improvement equally available to all so that all might avail themselves equally—*If* they wished to.

But though the historical explanation is history, it is no longer an explanation. For it is obvious to any-one—even to the most nostalgic—that times have changed and the obligations of governments with them. Governments, and particularly democratic governments, are no longer disinterested in matters affecting the education of their citizens. They have learned by observation that if they do not educate their citizens others will educate them. They have learned that if the citizens of a democracy are not taught the traditions of democracy they will be taught other traditions—and that they *can* be taught other traditions. They have learned that unless the citizens of a democracy are made to understand and then to value the history of democracy, and its litera-ture, and its science, they may not understand and may not value its democracy. For only those who understand and therefore value the civilization of democracy are able to understand why a democratic organization of society is preferable to other organi-zations of society which claim a superior efficiency: a superior force in war and a superior discipline in peace. Above all, only those who understand and therefore value the civilization of democracy are willing to defend democracy in their minds and in their beliefs against the persuasiveness of the ideal of Order as the end of life.

But it is not only because of the danger of propa-ganda to democratic governments that democratic governments now admit an affirmative interest in the education of their citizens. Democratic govern-ments have come to see in the last few generations of increasing population and increasing industriali-zation that democracy itself is a complicated and difficult business—the most complicated and the most difficult perhaps which men have ever undertaken. The self-government of a people under the most primitive conditions and in the smallest units, is difficult enough. The self-government of a people of many millions spread over an entire continent and engaged in the complicated activities of an industrial society is difficult beyond imagination. That difficulty all democratic peoples confess, and proudly confess, because it is the price of freedom. But in confessing the difficulty they admit also the need to overcome it. And since education is the only means of meeting difficulties of these proportions they admit also the necessity of education—education not only of the young but of the mature—education of the governors, the people, in the labor of self-government.

It is this question, then, which plagues the lay administrator of a national library in the present time: If democratic government now admits an affirmative interest in the education of the citizens, what then is the present obligation of the libraries democratic governments support? For libraries were instruments of education long before Carlyle said they were. Have government-supported libraries ceased to be the "poor men's universities" they were patronizingly called a generation ago, and become people's universities? And if they have become people's universities, what are their obligations to the people? Can they continue to feel that they have satisfied their obligations to the people if they wait for such readers as may care to come? Can they continue to feel that they have satisfied their obligations to the people if they offer every facility to scholars who will make, from the books in their collections, other books to be added to other collections? Or have they too an affirmative and urgent obligation—a positive duty—the duty and obligation of the university to interpret between the books and those who need them? And if they have this affirmative obligation to bring the record of the people's civilization to the understanding of the people, how are they to accomplish it?

These are the questions which a layman in this great profession comes to ask himself. They are questions doubtless to which men of professional experience will have their answers, some of one kind and some of another. Some will maintain, as certain journalists have already maintained, that it is a perversion of the whole idea of a library to suggest that libraries owe an affirmative obligation to the people. Others will perhaps reply that it is impossible for libraries in such a time as this to evade that obligation, that it is impossible for libraries in such a time as this to wait inside their walls for men to come to them, that libraries must now make use of every means at their disposal to bring to the people of this country a disinterested informed account of the means of education at their disposition. There will be those who will add that the people have a right to demand such service: that they have as much right to know from public servants what books are pertinent to their problems of self-government as to know from public servants what jellies they should conserve, what seed they should plant and what hen mash will produce eggs.

For myself I can say only this: that I do not believe libraries, any more than any other institution created by men, can be set above change; that librarianship, like every other human activity, must be continuously reinvented if it is to live; and that none, or so it seems to me, are under heavier responsibilities to the present than those whose profession is to conserve the past.

Of the
librarian's profession
· 1940

Nothing is more difficult for the
beginning librarian than to discover in what
profession he is engaged. Certain professions define themselves. Others are defined by those who
practise them. The librarian's profession is of neither
nature. A librarian is so called not for what he does,
as the farmer who farms or the lawyer who laws, but
from the place in which he does it. And the definitions of the librarians, though they are eloquent in
describing the librarian's perfections, are reticent in
saying what the librarian's perfections are for.

Hugo Blotius, the sixteenth-century librarian of
the Hofbibliothek in Vienna, defined his profession
by saying that a librarian should be learned in languages, diligent, and quiet — adding by way of re-
minder to his master, the Emperor, that "if not of
noble blood he should be given a title to enhance the
dignity of his office." Cotton des Houssayes told the
general assembly of the Sorbonne in 1780 that when
he reflected "on the qualifications that should be
united in your librarian" they presented themselves
to his mind in so great a number, and in such character of perfection, that he distrusted his ability not
only to enumerate but even to trace a true picture of
them. Pressing himself to the point, however, the

learned orator (who spoke, it should be noted, in the Latin tongue) supplied the following description of the office: "Your librarian should be, above all, a learned and profound theologian; but to this qualification, which I shall call fundamental, should be united vast literary acquisitions, an exact and precise knowledge of all the arts and sciences, great facility of expression, and lastly, that exquisite politeness which conciliates the affection of his visitors while his merit secures their esteem."

One gathers that M. des Houssayes thought well of the librarian's office, but beyond that, and a certain conviction of personal inadequacy, one is little wiser than before. To be at once a profound and learned theologian, the possessor of vast literary acquisitions, the exact and precise master of all the arts and all the sciences, a facile writer and a charming gentleman possessed of that exquisite politeness which wins heads as well as hearts, is to be an unusual and admirable human being—but even to be all these things at once is scarcely a profession.

And yet it is largely in the vein of the orator of the Sorbonne and the librarian of the Hofbibliothek that the profession of the librarian is presented. Modern librarians—perhaps because they do not speak in Latin—have never been as eloquent as Cotton des Houssayes, but even modern librarians write as though the profession of the librarian had been defined when the scholarly attainments and linguistic achievements of the, perhaps, ideal librarian have been described.

The consequence is that the beginning librarian is thrown upon his own resources, upon the dictionary, and upon the familiar sentences of the great founder of the Bodleian Library at Oxford. From Sir Thomas Bodley, besides learning that a librarian should not be "encumbered with marriage nor with a benefice of cure" and that he should be "a personable scholler and qualified, if it may be, with a gentlemanlike speeche and carriage . . . able to interteine commers in aswel of other nations as our owne, with meete discourses for the place," the apprentice librarian will learn that a librarian is a Keeper of a library. From the dictionary he will learn that a library is "a large collection of books, public or private." And by his own resources he will attempt to deduce what the Keeper of a large collection of books, public or private, may, in actionable and intelligible language, be. Keeper, but how a keeper? Of books—but what, then, in this context is a book?

It is not an altogether simple question, and for this reason. There are two meanings of the word "book" and two relations, therefore, between a book and the man entrusted with its keeping. There is one meaning which signifies a physical object made of certain physical materials in a physical shape. There is another meaning which signifies an intellectual object made of all materials or of no materials and standing in as many shapes as there are forms and balances and structures in men's minds. The two meanings overlap and are confused. Readers associate the intellectual book with the physical book, thinking of Plato's vision of the world in terms of dark green linen and a gilded name. Collectors associate the physical book with the intellectual book, imagining that because they possess a rare edition of a poet's work they somehow have possessed the poem. But the two meanings are nevertheless distinct. The physical book is never more than an ingenious and often beautiful cipher by which the intellectual book is communicated from one mind to another, and the intellectual book is always a structure in the imagination which may hang for a time above a folio page in ten-point type with a half-calf binding only to be found thereafter on a different page above a different type and even in another language.

When it is said, therefore, that a librarian is a keeper of books, it must be determined first of which of these two books he is the keeper. Is he, for one example, the keeper of the small, cloth-bound object of 110 pages of text and vi of front matter manufactured by Macmillan and Co., Limited, in London in 1928 and called *The Tower* by W. B. Yeats? Or is he the keeper of that very different object created in many men's minds before, and now in yours, by this—these words, these symbols, images, perceptions:

> That is no country for old men. The young
> In one another's arms, birds in the trees,
> —Those dying generations—at their song,
> The salmon falls, the mackerel-crowded seas,
> Fish, flesh or fowl, commend all summer long
> Whatever is begotten born and dies.
> Caught in that sensuous music all neglect
> Monuments of unaging intellect.

It makes a difference whether the book is the cloth and paper or the intellectual image. If it is the physical book of which a librarian is keeper, then the character of his profession is obvious enough. He is a custodian as all keepers of physical objects are custodians, and his obligations are a custodian's obligations. He is a sort of check boy in the parcel room of culture. His duty is to receive the priceless packages confided to him by the past and to redeliver them to the future against the proper stub. To perform that obligation he must be reliable, orderly, industrious, and clever. He must devise infallible and complicated ticket systems to find the parcels on the shelves. He must read the notations of origin and ownership in a dozen tongues. He must guard the wrappers from the risks of time and theft and matches and men's thumbs. He must be courteous and patient with the claimants. And for the rest he has no duty but to wait. If no one comes, if no one questions, he can wait.

But if it is not the physical book but the intellectual book of which the librarian is keeper, then his profession is a profession of a very different kind. It is not the profession of the custodian, for the intellectual book is not a ticketed parcel which can be preserved by keeping it from mice and mildew on a shelf. The intellectual book is an imagined object in the mind which can be preserved only by preserving the mind's perception of its presence. Neither is the librarian's profession the profession of the check boy who receives and guards and redelivers,—receives from the past, guards against the present and redelivers to the future,—for the intellectual book is not a deposit of the past which the future has a right to call and claim. The intellectual book is a construction of the spirit, and the constructions of the spirit exist in one time only—in that continuing and endless present which is Now. If it is the intellectual book rather than the physical book of which the librarian is keeper, then the profession of the librarian is not and cannot be the neutral, passive, negative profession of the guardian and fiduciary, but must become instead the affirmative and advocating profession of the attorney for a cause. For the intellectual book is the Word. And the keepers of the Word, whether they so choose or not, must be its partisans and advocates. The Word was never yet protected by keeping it in storage in a warehouse: the preservation of the Word is now, as it has always been, a cause—perhaps the greatest—not, I think, the least in danger in this time.

It makes a difference, therefore,—a very considerable difference in the understanding of the librarian's profession,—which of these two meanings of the book is taken. Both are held. The librarian who asserts that the sole and single strength of his profession in a distracted world is its disinterested objectivity—meaning its negative and custodial detachment from the dangers which beset the Word—thinks of the book necessarily as a physical object on his shelves for which, in its intellectual aspects, he accepts no share of risk or credit. The library trustee or the moralizing editor who demands of librarians that they stick to the job of pasting on the labels and handing out the loans accepts, but with less honesty, the same assumption—less honesty because he speaks, not from love of the librarian's profession, but from hatred of the Word, and fear of its persuasions.

Those who love the power of the Word and who defend it take the opposite position. Shortly after William Dugard was released, through the efforts of John Milton, from Newgate prison, he published two letters by John Dury, deputy keeper in 1649 of the King's medals and library, which put the case with eagerness and passion: "For if Librairie-Keepers did understand themselves in the nature of their work, and would make themselves, as they ought to bee, useful in their places in a publick waie; they ought to become agents for the advancement of universal learning. . . . The end of that Imploiment, in my conception, is to keep the publick stock of Learning, which is in Books and MSS, to increas it, and to propose it to others in the waie which may bee most useful unto all. His work then is to bee a Factor and Trader for helps to learning, and a Treasurer to keep them, and a Dispenser to applie them to use or to see them well used, or at least not abused."

As between these two conceptions of the profession a man can choose only for himself and not for those who practise the profession with him. But there are, notwithstanding, certain considerations which even a novice among librarians may propose. The chief of these considerations is the nature of the times in which men live. In a different time from ours — such a time as men a generation ago considered natural and normal — it made relatively little difference whether a librarian behaved himself as a custodian of volumes or as a "Factor and Trader for helps to learning, and a Treasurer to keep them, and a Dispenser to applie them to use." A generation ago the Word, the life of the mind, the monuments of unaging intellect, were not under attack. It was agreed by all civilized nations, by all governments in power, that the cultural tradition was a common treasure, that truth was an end to be sought equally by all men, and that the greatest glory and final justification of human life was the creativeness of the human spirit. In such a world the librarian who considered himself a custodian, who devoted himself to the perfection of his catalogue and the preservation of his bindings, and who waited for the calls of those who had business with his collections, was not only prudent but entirely wise. There was no need for him to advocate the cause of learning or to assert the supreme importance of the contents of his library, for no one doubted the one or challenged the other. The librarian who presented himself in the years before the Great War as a champion of culture would have received the ironic welcome he deserved. What was required of him then (and what he practised) was discretion, dignity, and a judicial calm.

But the world in which we live is not that world. The world in which we live is a world that world would have believed impossible. In the world in which we live it is no longer agreed by all governments and citizens that truth is the final measure of men's acts and that the lie is shameful. There are governments abroad and there are citizens here to whom respect for truth is naïve—governments and individuals who, when it is proved they lie, have not been shamed "either in their own or in their neighbors' eyes." In the world in which we live it is no longer agreed that the common culture is a common treasure. There are governments abroad and there are citizens here to whom the common culture which draws the peoples of the West together is a common evil for which each nation must now substitute a private culture, a parochial art, a local poetry, and a tribal worship. In the world in which we live it is no longer agreed that the greatest glory and final justification of human history is the life of the human mind. To many men and many governments the life of the human mind is a danger to be feared more than any other danger, and the Word which cannot be purchased, cannot be falsified, and cannot be killed is the enemy most hunted for and hated. It is not necessary to name names. It is not necessary to speak of the burning of the books in Germany, or of the victorious lie in Spain, or of the terror of the creative spirit in Russia, or of the hunting and hounding of those in this country who insist that certain truths be told and who will not be silent. These things are commonplaces. They are commonplaces to such a point that they no longer shock us into anger. Indeed it is the essential character of our time that the triumph of the lie, the mutilation of culture, and the persecution of the Word no longer shock us into anger.

What those who undertake to keep the libraries must consider—or so it seems to me—is whether this profound and troubling alteration of the times alters also their profession. Granted that it was not only possible but desirable for the librarian to think of his profession in negative and custodial terms in the quiet generations when the burning of books was a mediæval memory, is it still possible for librarians to think of their profession in these passive terms in a time in which the burning of the books is a present fact abroad and a present possibility at home?

Granted that it was not only prudent but wise as well for the librarian to admit no positive, affirmative duty to the cause of learning in a time when learning was universally honored and the works of great art and great scholarship were admired monuments, is it still wise for librarians to admit no positive duty to learning in a time when governments abroad teach ignorance instead of knowledge to their people, and fanatical and frightened citizens at home would, if they could, obliterate all art and learning but the art and learning they consider safe?

In a division which divides all men, because it is a division drawn through everything that men believe, can those who keep the libraries — those who keep the records of belief — avoid division? In a struggle which is truly fought, whatever the economic interpreters and the dialectical materialists may say to the contrary, across the countries of the spirit, can those who hold those countries remain neutral? In an attack which is directed, as no attack in history ever was directed, against the intellectual structures of the books, can those who keep the books contend their books are only objects made of print and paper?

I can answer only for myself. To me the answer is not doubtful. To me the changes of the time change everything. The obligations of the keepers of the books in such a time as ours are positive obligations because they have no choice but to be positive. Whatever the duty of the librarian may have been in a different world and a more peaceful generation, his duty now is to defend — to say, to fight, and to defend. No one else — neither those who make the books nor those who undertake to teach them — is bound as he is bound to fight in their behalf, for no one else is charged as he is charged with their protection. No one as much as he must say, and say again, and still insist that the tradition of the written word is whole and single and entire and cannot be dismembered. No one is under obligation as he is under obligation to meet the mutilators of the Word, the preachers of obscurantism, the suppressors — those who would cut off here and ink out there the texts their prejudices or their parties or their churches or their fears find hateful. And these obligations are not obligations which are satisfied by negatives. The books can be protected from the preaching demagogues and the official liars and the terrorizing mob not by waiting for attack but by forestalling it. If the cultural tradition, the ancient and ever-present structure of the mind, can still be saved, it can be saved by reconstructing its authority. And the authority of art and learning rests on knowledge of the arts and learnings. Only by affirmation, only by exhibiting to the people the nobility and beauty of their intellectual inheritance, can that inheritance be made secure.

Some years before his elevation to the bench, Mr. Justice Brandeis referred to himself as "counsel for the situation." The librarian in our time, or so it seems to me, becomes the counsel for the situation. His client is the inherited culture entrusted to his care. He — he more than any other man — must represent this client as its advocate. Against those who would destroy the tradition he must bring the force of the tradition. Against those who would mutilate the monuments he must bring the beauty of the monuments. Against those who would limit the freedom of the inquiring mind he must bring the marvels of the mind's discoveries.

Keepers of books, keepers of print and paper on the shelves, librarians are keepers also of the records of the human spirit — the records of men's watch upon the world and on themselves. In such a time as ours, when wars are made against the spirit and its works, the keeping of these records is itself a kind of warfare. The keepers, whether they so wish or not, cannot be neutral.

The librarian
and the democratic process
· 1940

It would be a brave man and an optimistic man who would suggest at this hour that the events of the past few weeks and months have been anything but evil. Certainly it would be a very foolish librarian who would suggest that there was any countervailing circumstance to balance the armed successes of obscurantism and brutal force. But there is, I think, one consequence of all this evil which may perhaps be turned to good, and not least by those who keep the libraries of this country. No one can look at Spain, at Austria, at Czechoslovakia, at Poland, at Finland, at Denmark, at Norway, at Holland, at Belgium and at the situation in Europe of France and Great Britain without asking himself with a new intensity, a new determination to be answered, how our own democracy can be preserved.

And no one can ask with earnestness and intelligence how our own democracy can be preserved without asking at the very outset how his own work, his own activity, can be shaped to that end. Librarians will ask that question of themselves as others will. And asking it, they may perhaps arrive at certain conclusions as to themselves and their relations to the life of the country which will be valuable not

Address delivered before the American Library Association, 31 May 1940. First published in the *ALA Bulletin* 34:385–88 (June 1940).

54

only to the country but to themselves as well. Specifically they may perhaps arrive at certain conclusions as to the great question which, in speech and in silence, explicitly and implicitly, has troubled them so long—the question of their profession.

The wholly admirable attempt to put librarianship upon a professional basis, has, as I understand it, met this principal difficulty: that it has proved impossible to arrive at a common agreement as to the social end which librarianship exists to serve. Men are bound together in professions not because they speak in professional vocabularies or share professional secrets or graduate from professional schools. Men are bound together in professions because they devote themselves in common to the performance of a function of such social importance—a function so difficult, so particular, and so essential to the welfare of society—that it requires of necessity a discipline, a technique, and even an ethic of its own. The definition of that function in the case of librarianship has not proved easy. The social function of the medical profession is known to every member of that profession. The social function of the profession of the law was well known to lawyers in the years before the law became a business. But the ablest and most distinguished librarians declare without hesitation that they have not themselves arrived at a statement of the function of librarianship satisfactory to themselves, nor have their colleagues supplied the lack.

Agreements have been fragmentary

The literature of the subject, in so far as I have been able to consult it, would seem to bear them out. Librarians have apparently agreed at one time or another upon a description of their social usefulness, but their agreements have been fragmentary and of such a kind as to increase rather than to resolve the doubts of sceptics. At the time of the founding of this Association, for example, librarians seem to have thought of themselves as purveyors of a harmless sort of recreation which would entice the humbler citizens away from "the street, the saloon, and the low amusement places of the poor." (I quote from an article by Mr. Sidney Ditzion in the *Library Quarterly*.) Twenty years later this same Association published a pamphlet called *American Library Association Material for a Public Library Campaign* in which the Association gave its blessing to a series of quotations which Mr. Ditzion reprints. Mr. Andrew Carnegie is cited as holding the opinion that the purpose of a library is to "improve" the masses. Mr. Henry E. Legler supplies the view that the purpose of a library is to "furnish the ambitious artisan with an opportunity to rise." Mr. F. A. Hutchins is authority for the proposition that the purpose of a library is to give "wholesome employment to all classes for those idle hours which wreck more lives than any other cause." It is at least doubtful to my mind whether librarians would accept these descriptions of their usefulness today. And if they did, it would be even more doubtful that a professional function would have been defined. To provide harmless recreation in competition with the street and the saloon is not a profession: if it were, Hollywood would be a profession from producers and directors down to ticket takers and ushers in plum-colored regimentals. To give wholesome employment for those idle hours which wreck the young is not a profession. And neither, in any realistic and comprehensible sense, is the "improvement of the masses." There are many things essential to the "improvement of the masses," if we are to permit ourselves that patronizing phrase, which have no professional implications whatsoever.

Forced to reconsider our librarianship

Definitions such as these do not of course exhaust the field. There are many more besides. But definitions such as these taken together with the contemporary state of mind would seem to establish the fact that no generally accepted or acceptable definition of the function of librarianship has yet been found. It is to this situation that the disasters of the last few months and their effects upon the American mind would seem to have application. For the destruction of democratic governments in Europe forces us as librarians to reconsider our librarianship, not in a vacuum, and not in relation to ourselves, but in relation to a democratic society . . . and, more, in relation to a democratic society which stands in the face of very present dangers.

A newcomer entering the library scene cannot avoid the impression that some at least of those who have undertaken in the past the labor of putting librarianship upon a professional basis, began not with the inward function of librarianship but with the outward furniture of professionalism – the professional schools and the professional terms and the professional privileges. The kind of reconsideration which danger now forces upon us is a reconsideration which cuts beneath all this to the essentials of our work and of our lives. Today we ask ourselves not how we can prove that our profession is a profession, but what we can do to preserve and make effective the social institutions in which we believe. More briefly, we ask ourselves what we as librarians in a democracy can *do*. And in the answer to that question, if we can find it, we may also find the solution of the difficulty which has plagued us for many years. "Out of this nettle danger" said a brave man once. Out of this nettle danger we may pluck not only for our country but for our life's work a meaning it has never had before.

Implicit in the nature of the crisis

The relation of librarianship to the present and impending democratic crisis is not, I think, impossible to describe. On the contrary it is implicit in the nature of the crisis. What democracy as a way of government and a way of life now faces is the threat of a competing form of government, a competing way of life, which is more immediately efficient than democracy because it sacrifices to efficiency — to commercial efficiency and to military efficiency — every other consideration, whether of individual freedom or of moral loyalty or of human decency — which could in any way detract from efficient military or commercial operation. What democracy as a way of government and a way of life now faces, in other words, is this — the question whether it can survive in competition with a more efficient way of government and a more efficient way of life which achieves its efficiency precisely by suppressing and destroying and eliminating all those human values which democracy was created to achieve.

How are the people to be informed?

Can a form of government and a way of life, in which the basic decisions are made by the people themselves, in the people's interest, and after discussion and reflection, survive in competition with a form of government and a way of life in which the basic decisions are made in secret by a single will? This was the question the President of the United States presented to the Eighth Inter-American Scientific Congress. It is a question the events of the last few days have presented with ever increasing intensity to all Americans — and not least to those who keep the country's libraries. But to us the question is presented with a particularity and a specific meaning which absorbs all our thought. For the question to us is not the question of public action but the question of public information. If the basic decisions are to continue to be made by the people, and if they are now to be made by the people, not in conditions of peace with margin for error, but in conditions of threat and danger and imminent war with no margin of any kind, how are the people to be informed? How are they to be provided not only with knowledge of the new facts creating the specific issue to be decided, but also with knowledge of the relevant parts of the historical record which constitute the precedents for action? How are they to be provided with defenses against the special pleading — the propagandas — the new propaganda which now impudently tells them, with all the lessons of Europe spread out for them to see, that they need not act, that no one wishes to attack them, that if they will only delay, if they will only remain weak and silent and defenseless, they will be safe: that if they will only wish to keep out of war they can keep out of war — as Norway wished, as Holland wished, as Finland wished? How are they to be provided with the facts of record, the chapters of their own experience, the materials they must have and have quickly and in the most useful form if they are to decide well and decide wisely the issues upon which all the future hangs?

These are the questions which present themselves to us when we consider our lives and our work not in abstract but in relation to the danger in which democracy now stands. For it is we who are the keepers – the proud keepers – of these records of the experience of our people, these precedents for decision. And it is we, if it is anyone, who will devise means and establish ways to make these precedents available to those who need them. *What* means we will devise, what ways we will establish, it is not for me, the youngest in point of service among you, to attempt to say. I have no doubt the leaders of our profession have long considered this most obvious and most desperately pressing problem and have drafted proposals to submit to you. But of one thing I am sure – that however we answer these urgent, these insistent questions – whatever technical procedures we adopt – the necessity of facing this problem in these terms cannot help but advance our understanding of our work and of ourselves. For no one, I believe, can think of librarianship in the terms of this necessity without a reconsideration of its basic purpose. And no one can think of librarianship in these terms without concluding that the notions of librarianship sometimes held are less than adequate. If librarians accept a responsibility for the survival of democracy in so far as they can assure that survival, if librarians accept a responsibility to make available to the people the precedents for decision and for action in order that the people may govern by them – then librarians cannot satisfy that responsibility merely by delivering books from public libraries as books are called for, nor can they satisfy that responsibility in reference libraries merely by supplying scholars with the materials of scholarship. They must do far more. They must themselves become active and not passive agents of the democratic process. And they must think of their libraries not as patented machines to deliver to the asker the book he wants, their responsibility and obligation ending when the book is delivered to his hands. They must think of their libraries as organizations of intelligent and well-trained men and women qualified to select from the record in their keeping such materials as are relevant to the decisions the people must make and able to provide those materials to the people in a useful form. They must think of their libraries in other words not as books and catalogs with the men to serve them but as expert men to whom the books and catalogs are tools for the performance of a duty. They must think of their libraries as the director of a legislative reference service thinks of the books he uses, not as the director of a circulation service thinks of books—they must think, that is, as the director of a legislative reference service who serves not Congress only or a legislature, but a people.

That such a service would be as difficult to perform as it is difficult to define we must of course admit: democracy is difficult and in no aspect more so than in the provision of information and the preparation for action. But that such a service is impossible of accomplishment we will no more admit than we will admit that democracy is impossible of defense. To subject the record of experience to intelligent control so that all parts of that record shall be somewhere deposited; to bring to the servicing of that record the greatest learning and the most responsible intelligence the country can provide; to make available the relevant parts of that record to those who have need of it at the time they have need of it and in a form responsive to their need—surely these are not difficulties beyond the competence of the men and women who have constructed in this country one of the greatest library systems the world has seen.

There are dangers in such an undertaking. But there are dangers also—even greater dangers—in refusing to attempt it. And the rewards of success are rewards worth seeking. Not only would the cause of democracy, the cause we believe to be the cause of civilization, be served. But it is conceivable that the profession to which we belong might find in the process the definition of its function for which it has sought so long—a function as noble as any men have ever served.

The Library of Congress protects its collections · 1942

The Library of Congress took preliminary measures for the security of its collections well over a year ago. These measures were of four kinds:

1. Survey of the collections to ascertain which materials should be removed to places of security in case of danger; which should be stored in places of relative safety within the library buildings; and which would be required for continuing services to Congress, the Federal agencies, the library world, and the general public, which the library will continue to render throughout the emergency, regardless of danger.

2. Location and designation of depositories in nonstrategic communities outside of Washington.

3. Arrangements for removal of materials: designing and procuring packing cases, planning procedures of removal, establishing priorities of transportation, organizing personnel, etc.

4. Submission of an estimate to Congress for funds to carry out the plans when made.

The operations described under heading (1) were performed during the months of January and February of last year. Anyone who has lived among books will appreciate the amount of labor and time required to survey and evaluate a collection of six mil-

First published in the *ALA Bulletin* 36:74–75, 144 (February 1942).

lion volumes, together with many more millions of maps, prints, manuscripts, and pieces of music for the purpose of discriminating between materials of foremost, and those of lesser, value. Many considerations must enter into a determination of the criteria upon which such an evaluation is based – importance to the American record, irreplaceability, association value, commercial value, value as source material for research, etc. (For example, are the papers of George Washington less valuable than those of a little-known Secretary of the Treasury, because the former have been published, while those of the latter will forever remain unprinted?)

Of course, neither I nor my colleagues would contend that our decisions were in all cases right; certain selections were necessarily arbitrary. Nevertheless choices were eventually made, and lists were prepared to facilitate withdrawal, packing, shipping, and recording should an occasion ever arise. This work was performed partly during regular library hours but for the most part out of regular hours and on a volunteer basis. To accomplish it some seven hundred members of the staff volunteered their services, and nearly five hundred volunteers contributed approximately ten thousand man-hours of overtime work to make this census. Accounts of the results of this census of the collections, written by Jerrold Orne, have been published.[1]

Search for depositories

The operations noted under heading (2) were relatively simple. When it became apparent that no plans

[1]Orne, Jerrold. "The Library of Congress Prepares for Emergencies." *ALA Bulletin* 35:341–48, June 1941; and *Report on the Precautionary Measures Regarding Its Collections, Adopted by the Library of Congress.* [Washington] June 1941. 25p. Mimeographed.

were being formulated to provide bomb-resistant shelters for the common storage of Federal records, books, art objects, museum pieces, etc., we instituted a search for dry, well-constructed depositories in nonstrategic inland areas outside of Washington upon which the library might depend in the event of an emergency. Due to the generous cooperation of public-spirited librarians and college administrators this search was successful. While the national interest requires that they remain for the present strictly anonymous I cannot forbear to make this preliminary acknowledgment of my deep sense of gratitude for their unfailing helpfulness.

As to the operations noted under heading (3), packing cases presented the first and most urgent problem. Realizing the great number of containers which would be necessary for shipment, we looked for a box which would be durable, inexpensive, reusable, and (for economy of storage when not in use) collapsible. Such a box was finally discovered. It resembles a container used by the British Museum under similar conditions. It is a collapsible, plywood container with metal joints and bands, reusable approximately a score of times, manufactured by the Atlas Plywood Corporation of Boston. Two standard sizes were selected (their dimensions are twelve by eighteen by thirty inches and twelve by twenty-four by thirty-two inches) which conform to requirements for shipment of 99 per cent of our materials. Special containers in outside sizes were made in our own workshops for other materials, and additional special containers, designed for hermetic sealing, were made for documents and books of the highest value.

Grant for project

Operations under heading (4) were as follows: On March 24, 1941, I submitted to the Bureau of the Budget an estimate in the amount of $150,000 to enable the library to effect the plans thus made. This estimate was eventually reduced at our request to $30,000, and was granted in that amount. Thereby we have been enabled to carry out the preliminary parts of the plan, including the procurement of containers, and partially to undertake shipment.

The library was therefore in a position on December 7, 1941, to take affirmative action. I am happy to be able to report that our principal treasures are already in places of security. The originals of the Declaration of Independence, the Constitution of the United States, the Articles of Confederation, the Lincoln Cathedral copy of Magna Carta (committed to our custody "for the duration") and the St. Blasius – St. Paul copy of the Gutenberg Bible – these and other materials beyond value, are in the safety of an inland repository many miles from Washington, under maximum security against any dangers now anticipated. Still other treasures – maps, manuscripts, rare books, prints, music, and even certain of our irreplaceable catalogs have already left us under guard for places much less likely than Washington to be attacked from the air. Additional materials are now in course of shipment.

I need not add, I am sure, that the Library of Congress will not permit these measures to interfere more than need be with the public services of which the library is so proud. It has been necessary, during the period of shipment, to close parts of the library buildings earlier in the day than is ordinarily the case. At the same time, however, we initiated (on the very day when hostilities began) a twenty-four-hour service for members of Congress and for government agencies, and we hope shortly to provide a general service, specially adapted to the emergency needs of the government, which in terms of wartime usefulness will more than counterbalance the temporary withdrawal of certain priceless treasures. I believe all librarians will join me in declaring that although libraries may be driven underground by the enemies of freedom, they will never be driven out of action. Indeed "One-Book" Hitler and his friends may find in time that libraries are weapons more dangerous to their hopes than planes or guns or submarines.

The Library
of Congress and national
defense · 1942

I am grateful for the opportunity you
have given me to comment on the work of
the Library of Congress and its relation to other
libraries during the present crisis.

It has been argued that the American people probably discovered the importance of literature to defense during the Revolutionary War, when a little
band of Continental troops, their ammunition ex-
hausted, rammed hymnbooks in their cannon and
fired them at the invading Hessians. But whatever
the origin of the discovery may have been there can
be no doubt that today government and science and
industry alike are dependent in large measure on the
literary resources of the country for efficiency in the
great and common task, the national task, of defense. Nor can there be any doubt that in this emergency librarians everywhere have accepted a grave
responsibility.

There are now in Washington about two hundred
and fifty government agencies serviced by the Library of Congress, and most of them (perhaps all of
them) are concerned directly or indirectly with defense. We are meeting their needs in various ways;
by preparing special bibliographies, by providing
them with rooms for the conduct of research, by
making special deliveries to their offices, by a sepa-

First published in the *Massachusetts Library Association Bulletin* 31:38 (June 1942).

rate unit to supply their orders for books, and by the establishment of new services such as the Radio Project and the study of Wartime Communication. A section of the Legislative Reference Service has been organized to compile digests of enacted, pending and proposed legislation connected with defense and to assemble and abstract current materials related to it.

But not only from Washington have come increased demands upon our service; requests for interlibrary loans are more numerous than ever before; orders for the photoreproduction of materials in our collections are mounting daily; the Card Division is supplying printed catalog cards at cost to the camp libraries; and the Division of Bibliography has compiled and distributed thirty five lists of references on various phases of defense.

One of the most important developments of recent months has been the establishment of the Experimental Division of Library Cooperation. Financed for a period of one year by the Carnegie Corporation, and headed by Herbert A. Kellar, archivist and historian, its broad objectives may be stated both negatively and affirmatively. Negatively it has as its purpose the coordination of the activities of American libraries by such methods as will eliminate waste and competitive action. Affirmatively it will seek to coordinate the activities of American libraries in such a way as to make their resources, considered as a whole, adequate to the needs of American scholarship. Affirmatively also, it will endeavor to bring about such improvement as can be effected by cooperative effort in the various services and technical functions of libraries – as, for example, the regional storage of books, the exchange and loan of reproductions, the cataloging of materials, book purchases, and the photocopying of manuscripts and unique books. It is a large scale undertaking, but, in my opinion, nothing less than a large scale undertaking would be useful. There are infinite possibilities to the services which libraries, working together, can perform for the American people. There is ample evidence of this; the Guide to Library Facilities for National Defense, prepared by the Joint Committee on Library Research Facilities for National Emergency is evidence, the publication of the Library of Congress Cooperative Bibliographies is evidence, and our own experience with other libraries is evidence, for we have learned that when our resources are inadequate we can appeal to other libraries for help, and help will be forthcoming. The response to those many appeals, sometimes for loans, sometimes for the reproduction of materials, has been unfailingly generous and encouraging and efficient. I believe the American people can expect their libraries to give a good account of themselves in any battle of the books.

The strongest
and the most enduring
weapons · 1942

This meeting is almost an anniversary. It lacks four days of being the ninth anniversary of the Nazi bonfire of May 10, 1933 in which 25,000 books were burned.

I mention that fact not because historical coincidence is particularly important—not because the day of the bonfire of books in Berlin was the tenth of May and the day of this booklovers' dinner in New York is the sixth—but because both occasions were remarkable for the same reason: both were tributes to the power of the book.

More particularly I mention them together because, in a certain and very compelling sense, the bonfire of Berlin was the greater—if unintended—tribute. And because certain consequences follow from that fact.

The Nazis—the misled and ignorant boys, the frustrated generation which made up the Nazi rabble, which became the Nazi gang, which produced the Nazi "Order"—these Nazis perpetrated their obscene and spiteful act because they knew, ignorant and disappointed and defeated as they were,

Address delivered before the American Booksellers Association. 6 May 1942. First published in *Publishers' Weekly* 141: 1810–14 (16 May 1942). Reprinted by permission of R. R. Bowker Co., a Xerox company, copyright © 1942 by R. R. Bowker Co.

that books are weapons and that a free man's books – such books as free men with a free man's pride can write – are weapons of such edge and weight and power that those who would destroy the world of freedom must first destroy the books that freedom fights with.

The question I should like to pose to you tonight – the question all of us who live with books, writers as well as booksellers, publishers as well as librarians, professors as well as public servants – must pose to ourselves is this: do we, for all our protestations – do we, for all our talk of books and all our labor with books and all our knowledge of books – do we recognize the power of books as truly as the Nazi mob which dumped them on a fire – do we truly and actually, in our lives as well as in our words, ascribe as great an influence to the books we write and publish and sell and catalog and teach, as those who fear the free men's books enough to burn them?

I am not indulging in rhetoric. I am asking a question. And I am asking it with the greatest seriousness of which I am capable. I think I know the answer. I think you know it, too. But you will agree with me that a devil's advocate could give us, if he wished, an uncomfortable half hour.

A competent devil's advocate could ask us to forget the brutality and ignorance of the Nazis for a moment and think back over our own behavior in the last decades to say whether, in our honest judgment, we who dealt with books during this period had acted as though we thought of books as powerful influences – as instruments by which the lives of men and nations can be shaped – or whether, on the contrary, we thought of books as merchandise – as packages to be sold alongside of rubber tooth brushes and bottles of hair tonic and packages of proprietary pills. It would not be an easy question to answer. We could reply in all honesty that the methods of merchandizing developed in the twenties and practiced in the thirties sold quantities of books such as had never before been sold and carried best-seller after best-seller over previous best-seller records until there seemed to be no limit to possible best-seller sales. But our devil's advocate, when we told him we had sold such quantities of books, could ask "What books?" "And selected for sale by what standards?" "And to what effect?"

"Certainly," he could say to us, "all questions of literary merit aside"—(and I assume we should be only too happy to leave them aside)—"all questions of literary merit aside, there was as little in these books themselves as in your handling of these books to indicate that you thought of books as powerful influences on the nation's life or on the nation's future. If ever the people of a great nation were ignorant of the secret changes of the world in which they lived—if ever the people of a great nation were unprepared to face the gathering and unfamiliar dangers of an altered world—the people of this country were ignorant and unprepared when first the Nazis struck for power. A few books on the best-seller lists—books like Hemingway's 'For Whom the Bell Tolls'—books like Ed. Taylor's 'Strategy of Terror'—books like Bill Shirer's 'Berlin Diary'—were books about the actual world—books which, if believed, would have given the people of the country some understanding of the dangers they faced before those dangers materialized in bombers over Honolulu and dead men off the Atlantic Coast. But the great bulk of the book sales were sales of books which give no indication whatever of the actualities of our time—no indication that the history of the last ten years has been a history which could only end in mortal danger to ourselves—no indication that the fascist revolution in Spain was the beginning of a fascist war which put our lives also, our freedoms also, in mortal peril, or that the Nazi conquest of Czechoslovakia was a conquest aimed, not at the Bohemian mountains only, but at other and more distant countries and eventually our own."

There is no reason to push the imaginary colloquy further or to make the obvious debaters' points on the other side: the point that American writers as a group were the earliest and the most courageous fighters against fascism in this country, exposing the Franco revolution in Spain for what it was when few beside the writers were willing to do so; the point that many American publishers devoted more time and money than they had to spare to the publication of anti-fascist books; the point that there were booksellers who undertook as a patriotic duty the forewarning of the people. All of these points can be made and others besides. But the fact nevertheless remains that the record as a whole is not a record of effective use of books for a purpose for which books could have been, and should have been, effective.

All of us, I think, will now agree that the American record over the last two decades is not a satisfying record. All of us will agree that the chain of folly linked to folly leads back from the tragic day when Bataan surrendered — the tragic day of the fall of Corregidor — to the no less tragic days when we let our victory in the last war fall from our irresponsible and foolish fingers. All of us will agree that the history of the last twenty-four years can now be seen, in retrospect, to unfold from irremediable negligence to inevitable disaster with the terrible and insistent fatality of a poem by Euripides. All of us will agree that there is no man or group of men of our generation — above all no man or group of men of those who deal with books — who can escape responsibility for the evil which has fallen on our time.

But what needs to be done now is not to look backward and confess our faults, what needs to be done now is to translate this general sense of responsibility into the single and specific responsibilities of single and specific men with single and specific duties. And to translate those specific duties into specific action. It is not enough, for example, for the motion picture industry to condemn those who assured it two and three and four years ago that its only job was to produce entertainment for the customers, letting death and the raven wheel above the electric signs on the theatre marquees. It is necessary now for the motion picture industry to face the facts and accept the conclusions — to face the fact that the pictures it makes are powerful influences upon the life of this nation; to face the fact that the influence of its pictures will be exerted whether it wishes to exert that influence or not; to face the fact that an escapist picture, a self-deluding picture, exerts an influence as inevitably as a true picture, a picture of actual things — and that its influence is escapist and delusive; to face the fact that the attempt of the industry to escape responsibility for the formation of American opinion by protesting that it had no relation to the formation of opinion — that it was merely engaged in providing entertainment to the American people — is a protest without truth or merit; to face the fact that the motion picture industry bears a primary and inescapable responsibility, along with the radio and the press and the book trade and the colleges and the schools, for the failure of the American people to understand long long before they came to understand it, the nature of the world they lived in and the dangers which that world presented.

There is no such distinction between entertainment on the one side and influence on the other as the motion picture industry once attempted to draw. The attempt to present the world as it isn't is as much an action influencing opinion as the attempt to present the world as it is, and "The Grapes of Wrath" or "The Spanish Earth" are no more "propaganda pictures" than the most illusory of the Hollywood contraptions which conceal the actualities of a tragic and endangered generation behind forests of pretty legs and acres of gaudy faces. If anything, the legs and gaudy faces are the more surely and more precisely "propaganda," for the world — or rather the non-world — they represent is the world in which a great part of the American people had drowsily come to believe — until the bombs fell and the silver screen was shattered and the mortar and bricks of the theatre itself showed through.

But what is true of the motion picture industry is true also of those who concern themselves with books — and, among them, with those whose concern with books is their distribution to the men and women who will read them. The book trade has its share of the responsibility which we all must carry and the book trade, as much as the motion picture industry — as much as the writers and the librarians and the rest — and for very similar reasons, must accept its share of blame. The philosophy of distribution adopted during the twenties and the thirties by the book trade had much the same effect upon the sale of books as the philosophy of distribution adopted by the motion picture industry had upon the output of motion pictures. The book trade also — though not so explicitly and not so audibly — insisted that it was merely engaged in selling merchandise the people wanted and that it accepted therefore no responsibility for the content of the packages it sold. Because books were sold in drugstores at cut rates, the men and women who sold them came to think of them in drugstore terms — in cutrate terms. A book was a $3.00 item or a 98¢ item and was sold as such. A book was famous because it had sold a hundred thousand copies or five hundred thousand or a million. Department stores stocked books the way they stocked dress-models — and for the same reason.

What was happening in the book trade, in other words, was about what was happening in the movies. But in the book trade, what was happening was more to be regretted. And for this reason — that the book trade, prior to the twenties, had been an institution which prided itself upon accepting precisely the responsibilities its subsequent practice tended to evade. The book trade had been, indeed, one of the most responsible of all the trades that men could practice. Books, in the last century and the century before, were sold by men who knew them, not as packages, but as books — men who had, and were entitled to have, opinions about the content and the value of the books they sold — men whose customers came to them, not to learn how many copies of a given novel had been sold before, but to talk about the novel itself — the innards of the novel — the quality of the book.

The tragedy was not so much the trend away from the old-style bookshop — though the trend away from it was sad enough. The tragedy was the decay of a function — a necessary function — a function essential to the dissemination of ideas in books. Books — true books — do not sell themselves. There is nothing about the externals of a true book, not even the most persuasive jacket, to make the readers who should read it want to take it home. True books are sold by the enthusiasm of those who know them and respect them. And that enthusiasm must express itself by word of mouth to count. The most eloquent review by the most esteemed reviewer will do little enough unless reader talks to reader. And of all possible readers, the bookseller who knows his books and knows his customers is the most persuasive talker. Without him the book trade becomes a trade indeed — a trade as impersonal as the trade in soap and soup—a trade of which the only voice is the full-page advertisement and the only measure the dollar-volume of commercial sales.

Until that function—the true bookseller's function—is restored to the selling of books it is not likely that books will play the part they must play in the shaping of our time, for it is not likely that the books which should reach thousands upon thousands of the citizens of this beleaguered republic will reach a fraction of that number. Books were never more important to this country than they are today. The questions which must be decided, the issues which must be resolved, are, many of them, questions and issues which only books can properly present. The profoundly searching questions, for example, of the order and form of the post-war world are questions for which books and books alone provide an adequate forum. And the basic question—the insistent question—of the true nature of the time in which we live is a question which demands the space and confines of a book. This time has not yet been discovered by the men and women who inhabit it and only the voyages of the most courageous books will show us what it is.

For many months, therefore—perhaps for many years—books will play a tremendously important, a deeply serious, role in the shaping of our history. And not alone the books of economic and political theory. Now as never before in centuries, the true labor of the art of words becomes an essential labor—the labor of the poet who holds experience before us in such a light, in such a posture, that the shape and meaning become visible and ardent—the labor of the novelist who reduces to order and to pattern the confusion and the incoherence of our lives.

The books will be written: have no doubt of that. The need of such a time as this brings out the books of which the time has need. But it is not enough to produce the books. It is not enough to have them reviewed in the columns of the few newspapers and magazines which undertake to review books seriously. It is necessary, if these questions are to be discussed by the vast public which must discuss them—it is necessary that such books as these should reach the hands of those who need them and who know they need them but do not know in practice how to satisfy the need.

Here then, if ever in the history of the modern world, is a task for the sellers of books—a task which the sellers of books alone can perform—a task which the bulk merchandisers of packaged print can never perform and should never attempt to perform. It is a task moreover which should fire the eye of any man who has the sense of history—a task to which any man could give himself with hope and pride. It is, in other words, precisely the task which the man who loves books and human beings enough to devote his life to mediation between the two will recognize as his.

It involves primarily the conscious acceptance of a difficult and arduous function—a function at once technical and universal—at once professional and human—the function of interpretation between the need of the people of our communities, and the literature of our time. To perform it a man must know them both as only the true bookseller can know them. A man must know the books of his time as a scholar knows his titles and he must know the people of his town as a doctor knows his patients. He must know, in other words, what his people need to learn and what his writers have to teach them. And he must bring his people and his books together: not *sub specie aeternitatis*—not under the aspect of eternity—but under the aspect of the time we live in—under this fiery and darkening and yet hopeful sky.

We in Washington can do a few things here or there to help you in this task. We can, for example, call to your attention the basic chart of the government's information activities—the chart drawn from the President's great Message on the State of the Union on January 6th. An account of this chart, describing these six objectives, will be mailed to you in the near future. It may serve you by showing you the principal objectives we have in mind. But the real task is one in which we can help you very little—one about which our knowledge and experience are very small compared to yours. The real job is a job which has to do with people—actual people, and books—specific books. You know your people better than we can ever know them. You know your books and their relation to your people. You and you alone can bring the two together.

I am no prophet, but if I were obliged to guess I should guess that the months immediately ahead will see a reversal of the tendency of the twenty years before and a resumption by the book trade of the position of high responsibility and professional authority it once occupied and occupied so well. If that happens—and it is for you to say whether it is to happen or not, for the people need it and the country hopes for it and the choice is yours—if that happens there will follow, I believe, an increase in the power and the influence of printed books such as this country has not seen before. If the coarse and brutal high school boys who made the Nazi bonfire could understand the power of a free man's books well enough to burn them, we in this country can understand the power of these books well enough to honor them and treat them as the things they are—the strongest and the most enduring weapons in our fight to make the world a world in which the free can live in freedom.

Toward
an intellectual offensive
· 1942

In the three months from December of last year to February of this the American mentality changed from defensive to offensive and an ultimate victory in the war became, in consequence, a probability instead of a desperate hope. Wars are won by those who mean to win them, not by those who intend to avoid losing them, and victories are gained by those who strike, not by those who parry.

What is true of the people as a whole in the war fought for the domination of the world should be true as well of the intellectuals — the writers and the scholars and the librarians and the rest — in the war fought for the countries of the mind. It should be true but isn't. The intellectuals have learned the first lesson of such wars: the lesson the nation learned belatedly at Pearl Harbor. They have learned that their scholar's country is in real and present danger. They have not yet learned the second lesson: the lesson the nation learned in the Dutch East Indies and the Philippines. They have not yet learned that their scholar's country can be saved and their world made habitable only by courageous and unrelenting attack.

The learning of the first lesson was long and diffi-

Address delivered before the American Library Association, 26 June 1942. First published in the *ALA Bulletin* 36:423–28 (July 1942).

cult enough as we can all remember. Down through the thirties to the invasion of Poland a considerable number of American intellectuals preached and practised an intellectual isolationism which was at least as frivolous, and certainly as blind, as the political isolationism of their political counterparts. They not only denied that their country of books and scholarship and art and learning was the principal target of the world revolution then fomented: they denied even that that country of theirs was in any danger or could possibly be attained or touched by the world-mob gathering against the sky. Their country, they informed us, was safe beyond its literary seas, its learned waters — safe from any war or any revolution. Art, they said, and books and learning of all kinds were things remote from wars, remote from revolutions. All the scholar, or the keeper of books, or the writer, or the artist, had to do was to stay on his own side of his particular ocean and tend to his own affairs and let the wars go by. The wars had always gone by before, they said, and the art had remained, the books had remained.

Down through the thirties to the invasion of Poland they went on like that. Not all of course. There were many writers who had looked at Spain and seen what they had seen. There were others who had looked at China. There were scholars who had looked in the books for the things actually lived, the things understood. Not all the American intellectuals of the years before the invasion of Poland were isolationists of the mind, inhabiters beyond imaginary oceans. But many were. And even after Poland there were still many. Until Denmark fell. And Norway fell. And Holland fell. And Belgium fell. And France fell. Then there were none — none but a few ghosts, the shrill inaudible voices.

Art and learning not a world apart

When you saw in country after country that it was the intellectuals, the artists, the writers, the scholars who were searched out first and shot, or sequestered first, or left to rot first in the concentration camps — when you saw in country after country that it was the books which were banned or burned or imprisoned, the teachers who were silenced, the publications which were stopped — when you saw all this, it was difficult to insist that the world of art and learning was a world apart from the revolution of our time. It was awkward, not to say embarrassing, to repeat over and over again that the world of books and paintings and philosophy and science was a world set off behind oceans no violence of war could ever cross successfully. It was even a little ridiculous to declare that this attack upon learning, this attack upon the whole world of the human spirit, was no affair of those who live by learning and the spirit — that their only duty was to turn their backs.

So that after the fall of France the first lesson was learned. What the bombs at Pearl Harbor did to the political isolationists, the murders of the Gestapo did to the isolationists of the spirit. It is difficult to argue that a bomb cannot fall or a man be killed in your country when the bombs have fallen and the dead men are on the beaches from Jupiter Light to Quoddy and on north. It is difficult to argue that the world of art and books and science is not endangered by a revolution which has already murdered the artists and the men of letters and the books.

The principal target

But the parallel between political isolationism and intellectual isolationism, though it holds in part, does not hold in full. Political isolationism in the United States was replaced by a defensive mentality, which was replaced in time by a mentality committed to attack. Intellectual isolationism was replaced by a defensive mentality only: the second transformation never followed. Scholars and writers admitted after Czechoslovakia and France and Norway that their country—the country of the mind—the country of the free man's mind—was indeed under attack and that their pretense of inviolability, of other-worldliness, was a pretense as unrealistic as it was unworthy. They admitted indeed that their country, the country they inhabited as scholars and as writers and as men of books, was the *principal* target of the revolution of our time—that this revolution was in fact as in word a revolution aimed against the intellect, against the mind, against the things of the mind—a revolution of ignorance and violence and superstition against the city of truth. They agreed in consequence that the city must be held, must be defended. But the second step, the second and essential step, the scholars and the men of letters have not taken even yet. They have not accepted the necessity of offensive war. They have not perceived that the defense of the country of the mind involves an affirmation, an assertion of a fighting and affirmative belief in intellectual things, a willingness not only to resist attacks upon their world and on themselves but to conceive offensives of their own and fight them through and win them.

Scholars have acted

A very large number of American writers have enlisted in one way or another in the war against fascism, some as soldiers, some as polemical writers, some as employees of the government. Scholars have put their scholarship at the service of their country and their country's cause, artists and musicians also. But it is in their capacity as citizens of the political, not of the intellectual, world that these men have acted. They have put aside their quality as writers and scholars for the duration of the war. They have said, in effect: "Our scholar's world, our writer's world is threatened: we will defend it on the political front, the front of arms – we will defend the city of the mind by defending the actual cities of our other world, the world we know as citizens and men."

It is a courageous thing to do and a necessary thing to do. The actual cities must be held and the physical battles for their safety must be fought and won at any cost, at any sacrifice. Certainly the enlistment of the scholars in those battles is a heartening and an admirable thing, just as the failure of men of scholarship and letters to oppose the rising Fascist revolution in the thirties was a shame to Western scholarship and a reproach our generation must accept. But courageous and necessary as these actions are they are nevertheless inadequate to the scholar's obligations. Whatever may be true of other cities, the city of the mind cannot be defended by deserting it to fight on other fronts. Above all it cannot be defended by deserting it when the ultimate objective of the forces which have made this war is precisely the destruction of that city.

To fail to understand that fact is to fail to understand the nature of the conflict in which our world is now engaged. This conflict is not a conflict which can be won by arms alone for it is not a conflict fought for things which arms alone can conquer. It is a conflict fought for men's convictions – for the things which lie beneath convictions – for ideas. The war of arms might end in victory on the Pacific and along the Channel and in the Mediterranean and in Africa and Asia, and the war might still be lost if the battles of belief were lost—above all if the battle to maintain the power and authority of truth and free intelligence were lost—if the confidence of men in learning and in reason and in truth were broken and replaced by trust in force and ignorance and super-stition—if the central battle for the preservation of the ultimate authority of mind in human living should be lost.

Battle can be lost

And that central battle can be lost. We shall deceive ourselves if we pretend that the attack upon intellectual things, the attack upon the things of art and of the spirit which has been a fundamental part of the maneuvers of our adversaries, has been unimportant in effect. On the contrary no single element of their propaganda has been more successful than the propaganda the Fascists have brought against the intellectual authority. And for an excellent reason. Which is this: that fascism is in its essence a revolt of man against himself—a revolt of stunted, half-formed, darkened men against a human world beyond their reach and most of all against the human world of reason and intelligence and sense.

Anti-intellectual propaganda

No propaganda was or could have been more powerful than the anti-intellectual propaganda of the Fascists because no propaganda responded more precisely to the prejudices and the emotional predispositions of those to whom the Fascist revolution made its principal appeal. The bankrupt merchants, the frustrated apprentices, the disappointed junior engineers, the licked, half-educated, unsuccessful clerks and journalists and discharged soldiers to whom the Fascist revolution called in every country where the Fascist cause made headway, were men sick of a profound, a deadly sickness—a sickness they had caught in the swarming, crowded, fetid, and unlovely air of the swarming and unlovely time which bore them—a sickness of which the name was ignorance and envy. For men whom ignorance and envy bred, no conceivable propaganda was more seductive than the propaganda which presented all learning, all enlightenment, all distinction of the man and mind as false and foolish.

For a generation to which the world had ceased to make either sense or loveliness or justice, a propaganda which belittled human intelligence and sneered at human morality was a propaganda which was believed before it was uttered. Defeated by a world which used them as tools but had no use for them as men, they turned, not on the world but on themselves—on man—on all those things in man which seemed to men before them to be admirable and of good repute but now to them seemed otherwise. The Fascist propaganda which tore down the intellectual authority, the moral rule, was not, in other words, *one* of the devices of the Fascist revolution—it *was* the Fascist revolution. For fascism is in essence nothing but the latest, saddest, most pathetic, and most hopeless form of the ancient revolution of mankind against itself—the recurring and always tragic effort of mankind to kill the best it knows in order to make peace with what is not the best—but would be if the best were dead.

It would be foolish therefore—indeed it would be worse than foolish—to pretend to ourselves that the attack upon our scholar's world is not a dangerous attack—an attack which has done injury already and can still do more. But certainly we have no temptation to belittle its effect. We know what harm has been done in other countries and in this as well. We know, for example, if we read the press or watch the signs in any medium, how deep the effort to destroy the confidence of men in learning and in intellectual things has gone. There was never a time, I think, in the history of this country when learning was held cheaper than it is today—or when the men of learning and of letters had less honor. A hundred and fifty years ago in America, or a hundred years ago, or fifty, a man of learning was honored for his learning. Today to be an intellectual is to be an object of suspicion in the public mind. To be a professor is to invite attack in any public service, any public undertaking. To be an artist is to live beyond the reach of serious consideration.

No need for proof

There is no occasion to produce testimony or to document the obvious. The evidence is so generally familiar that it passes without comment. When an attempt was made in an ill-attended session of the House of Representatives this last spring to cut the appropriation of the Library of Congress to such a point that the national library of the United States would have been unable to buy new books beyond its regular continuations and subscriptions—an attempt which might have succeeded had not the House and Senate by common and nonpartisan action reversed its initial success—when this attack was made upon a great symbol of learning, a great institution of scholarship, no public outcry was aroused. No public resentment was expressed even by those who might most readily have voiced resentment. There were two editorials, one each in the *New York Times* and in the *Washington Star.* And we—such is the humility of those these days who have the charge of learning—we were grateful for these two. And did what could be done with their support.

This angers you, my friends, to hear of now. It did not anger you then. And why? Because you never heard of it most likely. And why did you never hear of it? Because, neither to your friends nor to your newspapers nor to your radio commentators did it seem to have significance enough to call it to your notice. And why? The answer I think is obvious: it was not news. It was not news that an attack had been made upon an institution of learning: such attacks had been made before and frequently. It was not news that the leader of the attack had unconsciously revealed a fear of books, a fear of letting information reach the people, a fear of scholarship and learning; such fears had been revealed before and not least often by the very man the *Times* rebuked. Nothing in the sorry spectacle was news to anyone. Fifty years ago an attack upon a great library, an attempt to deprive the people of this country of their books, would have brought down upon the politician who attempted it a storm of criticism in the public press. Today it passes almost without comment.

Record known

But no citations of the evidence are necessary. You know the record for yourselves. You know what headway the propaganda aimed against the intellectuals has made. You know where you stand in this conflict—you and everything you care for. You know therefore whether it is possible to maintain as we and others like us have maintained so long, a negative position, a defensive mind.

For myself I do not think so. The city of learning — or so it seems to me — can be defended in this war only as the city of freedom can be defended: by attack. To realize that the world of books and learning and of art is the principal objective of those who would destroy our time, and to sit back in humble and defensive silence awaiting whatever onslaught they wish next to make, is the role, it seems to me, not only of cowardice but of foolishness as well. Like this America we love enough to fight for overseas on every continent, our scholar's country is a country we must fight abroad to save. Not by awaiting attack but by preventing it, not by resisting but by overcoming, can the towering city of the mind be victor in this war. And unless we are ready now or very soon to bring the battle to our enemies and overcome them — to strike down ignorance where ignorance appears — to fly our flag of truth and reason higher than our enemies can cut it down — we cannot win this war within the war on which the outcome of the war itself depends.

Library of Congress employee relations · 1943

I consider it a compliment—a compliment to the Library of Congress as a
whole—to be asked to report upon the Library's
employee-relations program. If the Library's program is interesting in conception, or successful in
practice, it is very largely because of the lively and
intelligent cooperation of the Library unions and
members of the Library staff. The Library's unions
are Local 28 (now Local 1) of the United Federal
Workers of America, and Local 626 of the National
Federation of Federal Employees. These two unions
and the Library's Staff Advisory Committee, a representative Committee of organized and unorganized
employees, took an active part in the negotiation of
the basic General Order, General Order 1177, on
which the Library's employee-relations program is
based. The final document, not only in substance but
in form as well, is as much their work as it is the work
of the Library Administration.

The general objective was agreed upon from the
start. Both the Administration and the staff of the
Library wanted a program which would provide
employees with ready access to supervisory officers
and administrative officers at all levels for the discussion of individual problems affecting employee
status and welfare, together with a procedure for the

First published in *Personnel Administration* 5:6–7 (May
1943).

handling of grievances which would assure to all employees an expeditious and impartial treatment of any complaints they might have. The difficulties were altogether difficulties of ways and means.

There was, for example, the essential problem—a problem unsolved so far as I know in government practice—of the nature of the relationship between administrative officers and members of the staff. Clearly the relation between administrators and staff members in government agencies is not the relation of employer and employee. The employer in government is the whole people, and administrative officers are therefore as much employees as those whose work they direct or supervise. Moreover, administrative officers work within statutory and other limitations which qualify their freedom of action in employee relationships as in other things. In the same way, non-administrative employees of the government are restricted in their employee activities by the fact that they work for the government, which is to say that they work for the whole people. But despite these differences, it nevertheless remains true that administrative employees do, within certain limits, exercise the ordinary employer function of hiring and firing, rewarding and punishing.

The definition of the relationship is thus not easy. The Library's statement of principles as drafted is based upon the proposition that administrative and non-administrative employees in the government service meet and work out their difficulties as employees in common of the whole people with a view to the interest of the people as a whole. Neither I, however, nor any other member of the Library staff claims that that form of words disposes of this most troublesome and basic of government personnel problems.

It will, perhaps, be helpful to follow briefly the steps taken in the drafting of General Order 1177. A previous Order, also worked out in large part in negotiations with the Library's unions, had been in force for something over a year. The first step in drafting the new Order was to inform the Library staff of the apparent defects in the existing Order and to invite comments and suggestions. Meantime, the Library's Personnel Office was directed to conduct a survey of the types of policies and procedures established in other Federal Agencies. The results of this survey were communicated to the staff, and a series of conferences with the Library's unions, the Staff Advisory Committee, and individual employees was thereupon scheduled. The result of these meetings was a series of drafts, each of which was submitted to the staff for comment either directly or through the various representative instruments, and made the basis for further conferences in my office.

The method was slow, requiring as it did something over five months to complete. It made heavy demands upon the time of the principal administrative officers of the Library, and not least upon the time of the Librarian. But the result was a gradual evolution of principles and of text in the progress of which a very considerable part of the staff participated. Indeed, I think it is quite accurate to say that every member of the staff of the Library with an active interest in the Library's personnel relations participated more or less continuously in the work of discussion and of drafting, either directly or through the representation of the unions and the Staff Advisory Committee. The final draft was not the work of technical experts, and it may suffer technically from that fact. It has, however, countervailing advantages in that it represents the best thinking of those most immediately involved in its operation.

We in the Library of Congress believe that we have gained more from the drafting of the basic Order than the basic Order itself. We have learned that personnel and administrative practices cannot be thought through in abstract. No policy-forming official, regardless of his ingenuity and foresight, can devise a program involving human elements without knowing those human elements in human terms. And the human terms are diverse and complex. The day to day supervisor of a small group of employees has problems peculiar to his duties which cannot safely be generalized beyond those duties. The chief of the large division, the bureau head, the head of an office, all have problems which are typical only of themselves. The interests of employees are as varied as their status in the organization. You have the organized employee, the unorganized, the temporary, the probational, the permanent, the clerical, the custodial, the professional, the full-time, the part-time, the aggressive, the reticent, and so on indefinitely. No one of these categories of employees can think in terms of all employees. Only a method of approach to personnel problems which takes human consideration of human differences can possibly hope to achieve even a modicum of success.

How much success the Library's program will achieve, time alone will tell. It has been issued on the explicit condition that its terms are to be re-examined at the end of another year. But whether it requires extensive redrafting at the end of that year or not—whether or not its provisions prove generally satisfactory—there is one thing of which we are certain: that we will know how to attack the problems its operation may present to us.

The intellectual needs of liberated peoples
· 1944

The labour of rebuilding—of restoration—at the end of this war will present difficulties of a character never before encountered in the history of warfare.

Not only will it be necessary to rebuild cities, reconstruct industries, repair transportation systems, and restore whole populations and peoples to their homes. It will be necessary also to reconstitute, in certain of the occupied countries, the entire fabric of intellectual intercourse—the nerve system by which ideas are communicated from one man to another and from one generation to the next.

It will be necessary, specifically, to provide educational systems to replace those destroyed or perverted by the Fascists, and to replace, in so far as it may be possible to replace them, the stores of printed books and works of art and scientific instruments burned or pillaged or mutilated by the invaders.

There have been conquerors before this generation whose armies burned and murdered and looted as they went. There have never before been conquerors whose armies burned and murdered and looted with a specific and calculated purpose to destroy the culture of conquered peoples in order that a desert of ignorance and apathy might receive a new and hateful culture in its place. With other conquer-

First published in the *Times* (London) 3 May 1944.

ors the destruction of libraries and the murder of intellectual leaders was an incident of military conquest. With the Nazis, military conquest has been a means to the murder of intellectual leaders and the destruction of libraries. The conquest at which the Nazis aimed was a conquest not of territory but of the minds and opinions of men—the ultimate conquest from which all other spoils of land and ores and industries depend.

The Nazi purpose has already been defeated. Eventually the Nazis themselves will be destroyed. But the evil they have done in the countries where their plans were carried out will live long after them. It is an evil, moreover, which will continue, long after the Nazis have disappeared, to threaten the peace of the world as they themselves threatened it. For it will perpetuate the condition they wished to bring about. So long as there remain great areas of the world where libraries and schools are lacking, there will remain areas where the anticulture which fears libraries and schools may well take root. To eradicate Fascism means to eradicate the conditions which produce Fascism. Of these, superstition and ignorance are not the least, nor the least dangerous.

But it is one thing to say that school systems must be re-established and libraries restored and quite another thing to recreate them. Libraries above all. A great collection of books is always and necessarily unique. It cannot be reproduced. The older books are no longer available for purchase. The newer, even when they still exist in dealers' stocks, are difficult to bring together. If the libraries of Poland have been destroyed as completely as we now believe—if libraries in France and the Low Countries are to suffer the fate of the library of the University of Naples—it will be impossible to repair the damage by the purchase of volumes. No sum of money, no matter how generously given, could secure the older basic library materials which, when they exist, exist in the collections of other libraries where they are not for sale.

The only practicable way of making materials of this kind available to people whose regional libraries have been destroyed is to give them access to materials in the collections of libraries of other regions. The only practicable solution, in other words, of the problem of library reconstruction in occupied Europe and Asia is to enable the scholars of these areas to draw upon the resources of the great libraries in other parts of the world which still possess their collections. If a system of world circulation of essential library materials were established, the reconstruction of the libraries of Poland, however difficult, would not be impossible. Materials still obtainable from publishers and book dealers could be purchased. Materials not obtainable by purchase would be provided by loan from the other parts of the world.

A world circulation scheme of this character presents obvious difficulties. It would involve the acceptance of the world's great libraries of the principle that the great libraries hold books in their possession as trustees, not for the people of their immediate neighbourhoods, nor even for the people of their particular countries, but for the entire generation of living men. But the principle of the universality of culture, of the right of all men to know and to understand the achievements of mankind, is not, after all, a novel principle, nor has any civilised nation ever seriously claimed to "own" privately and exclusively the works of literature and art and science in the possession of its libraries and galleries and museums. To give this generally accepted principle an affirmative rather than a negative application is not to change its meaning.

The practical difficulties are, if anything, less than the psychological. Libraries in various countries have long since perfected a system of so-called "inter-library loan" within national boundaries which works well and usefully. Air transport, rapidly developed during the war, can readily extend inter-library loan beyond national boundaries. In addition there are, of course, the photographic devices familiar to all librarians. Copies or micro-copies can be readily and cheaply made where original materials cannot be sent. The only new administrative machinery required would be an international clearing house which would not need to be either large or expensive.

The future implications of any such proposal are evident enough. A world circulation system for printed materials would involve eventually a division of responsibility between libraries on a world basis. If materials could be borrowed internationally in original or photocopy it would no longer be necessary for the great reference libraries of the world to aim at the unattainable goal of "completeness" in all fields and for all areas. Instead the great libraries could depend upon each other to cover in full and in detail the printed materials of their respective regions. The result would be to free the funds of the individual libraries for a more selective and a more feasible acquisitions policy. Having secured the necessary regional materials to fulfil their obligations, the balance of purchase funds could be spent not in a vain effort to cover the product of the world's presses but in pursuit of whatever scholarly purposes appealed most urgently at the time. The libraries of the United States, for example, would divide among themselves responsibility for the complete possession and ready loan of American materials, and would use the balance of their purchase funds to secure foreign materials of particular interest to them, trusting to the libraries of other regions to cover the printed materials of their areas in full and in detail and to make those materials available on loan when needed.

The reorganization
of the Library of Congress,
1939-44 · 1944

This paper, being a library paper, should begin with a warning to the cata-loger. The author is not Archibald MacLeish, though the by-line says so. The author is the Library of Congress. It would be almost impossible for the most gifted and persistent cataloger on earth, even though a member of the Library's staff (which she certainly would be), to identify the occasional sentences I have borrowed from the reports of my colleagues — Mr. Clapp, or Mr. Mearns, or Dr. Evans, or Mr. Henkle, or Dr. Hanke, or Mr. Rogers, or Mrs. Wright, perhaps, or other members of the Library's staff. The reorganization of the Library of Congress was a labor in common of many men and women, and this account of it is such a labor also. If the general orders and other documents in which the Library's organization was accomplished and expressed were generally in my words, it was not because the work was necessarily mine but rather because, being a writer rather than a librarian, I prefer the sound of my own phrases. If the manuscript of this paper is largely in my handwriting, it is merely because mine were the last hands through which it passed.

I insist on this not out of modesty but out of pride. Of the various changes accomplished in my five-year term, I am proudest of the change which has

First published in the *Library Quarterly* 14:277–315 (October 1944), published by the University of Chicago Press.

drawn into the active administration of the Library of Congress an increasing number of the members of its staff. A department of government is efficiently run when it is run by every man and woman in it, each directing the work he has to do, whether that work is done by many or by one, and that one himself. The Library of Congress has not yet achieved that ideal; but the professional forum, the staff advisory committee, the various operating committees, and the Librarian's Conference have carried it a long way forward. I could ask no greater assurance for the future welfare of the Library than its continuing development of these instruments and others like them.

But if the author of this paper is not what he seems, neither is the paper. It calls itself "The Reorganization of the Library of Congress, 1939-44." The implication is that the new Librarian of Congress, having just heard himself certified by the American Library Association as no librarian, took one look at the world's largest library and proceeded to reconstruct it from the ground up. Nothing of the kind, I need hardly say, happened. I did not set out to reorganize the Library of Congress, any more than I had set out to become its Librarian. The American Library Association was quite right. I knew nothing about library administration as such in 1939. To be entirely frank, I am not sure that I know much more about it today, for I am even more doubtful now than I was then that the administration of a library differs essentially from the administration of any other organization in which highly developed skills and highly developed personalities are combined in a highly complicated undertaking.

What actually happened in 1939 and 1940 and thereafter was merely this: that one problem or another would demand action; that to take action it would become necessary to consider the effect of the proposed action on related situations; that related situations had, in turn, their related situations; and that eventually it would prove simpler to change several things than to change one.

The reason will be obvious to anyone familiar with the Library as it then was. The Library of Congress in 1939 was not so much an organization in its own right as the lengthened shadow of a man—a man of great force, extraordinary abilities, and a personality which left its fortunate impress upon everything he touched. Only a man of Herbert Putnam's remarkable qualities could have administered an institution of the size of the Library of Congress by direct and personal supervision of all its operations, and only he if his administration were based upon the intimate familiarities of forty years. To succeed Mr. Putnam—if one may speak of succeeding a man who did not have, and never could have had, a successor in the accurate sense of that term—to succeed Mr. Putnam was a good deal like inheriting an enormous house at Stockbridge or Bar Harbor from a wise, well-loved, strong-minded, charming and particular uncle who knew where everything was and how everything worked and what everyone could do but had left no indications in his will.

My first reaction to the Library of Congress—and my last may well be the same—was the conviction that I owed it to my successor to leave him an organization with a momentum of its own. The principal difficulty with the old Library, from my point of view as the unexpected and unexpectant heir, was the fact that the whole fabric depended from the Librarian as the miraculous architecture of the paper wasp hangs from a single anchor. There was the Librarian—myself—in his vaulted office with his messenger outside. There was the chief assistant librarian, the late regretted Martin Roberts, in a room across the hall, his desk piled with order slips and vouchers. There was the office of the secretary of the Library—for neither the Librarian nor the chief assistant librarian had a full-time secretary of his own. And below these two, dependent on them for immediate supervision and direction, were thirty-five different and separate administrative units engaging in activities as various and diverse as the administration of the national copyright laws, the conduct of chamber-music concerts, the procurement of talking books for the adult blind, the cataloging of books, the care of the Library buildings, the provision of reference and research service to the Congress, the publication and sale of cards to other libraries, the purchase of library materials, the service of manuscripts and rare books and prints to readers, the recruiting of personnel, and the provision of learned information in most of the languages of the world to readers everywhere.

The so-called Librarian's Committee (Messrs. Joeckel, Rice, and Osborn) which examined the Library at my request a few months after my appointment described this situation in the chill vocabulary of the science of management by calling it

in all probability the largest and most diffused span of control to be found in any American library . . . Small wonder that the Library of Congress is often described as a group of libraries within a library. It is in effect a loose federation of principalities, each with strongly developed traditions and with administrative and technical idiosyncrasies. . . . There can be little doubt that the steady expansion of the number of independent organization units is in large measure responsible for many of the present difficulties in technical operations as well as in administration of the Library. Almost of necessity, each division has made its own decisions as to the technical apparatus of catalogs, shelflists and indexes it has devised and as to its relations to the processing operations of the rest of the Library. It is not surprising that a considered program for the institution as a whole has not been developed.

At the beginning, needless to say, there was no question in my mind of "a considered program for the institution as a whole." There was merely the question of survival. Every personnel action, every voucher, every book order, and much of the Library's correspondence, except for the most routine communications, required in theory the Librarian's signature. Since I have a constitutional disinclination to signing documents I do not know to be right, and since the Librarian in his painted vault had no possible means of knowing whether the greater part of the papers he was expected to sign were correct or not, the situation was difficult—not to say downright impossible. Knowledge was separated from responsibility, and responsibility from knowledge. Signatures which should have been substantial authentications had become mere formalities. Because the fiscal officers of the Library, like the Library's great disbursing officer, the late Wade H. Rabbitt, were men of conscience, industry, and skill, the Library's accounts were in good shape; but the officer who so declared them over his signature had no means of knowing that they were without turning himself into a chief clerk or accountant.

The practice would have been unsatisfactory anywhere. In the Library of Congress it was entirely unacceptable. The Library's fiscal operations are complicated, diverse, and difficult to control at best. It not only accounts for appropriations which amounted in 1939 to $3,107,707 and which have now reached $4,326,930. It disposed as well of $350,000, this last year, from nongovernmental sources, $75,000 of which came from its own investments. It operates two businesses which gross better than $300,000 each per annum—the Copyright

Office and the sale of catalog cards. And it administers two revolving funds in its photoduplication service and its recording laboratory which supports annual sales of about $75,000 and $18,000, respectively. Some indication of the complexity of the Library's fiscal operations and procedures is provided by the fact that a staff of five highly competent investigators from the general accounting office, who began a survey of these operations at my request in the fall of 1939, were unable to file their final report until April 1942. Some indication of the character of those operations at the time is given by a preliminary report of a representative of the division of administrative management of the Bureau of the Budget, who stated in a "Memorandum on Fiscal Administration in the Library of Congress" that "in view of the present inadequacy of the fiscal facilities of the Library and a lack of co-ordination of its several fiscal activities, a complete reorganization appears to be necessary."

What was true of fiscal operations was true of other operations of the Library. With the exception of the administration of buildings and grounds, which was centered in a superintendent, most of the Library's administrative operations were performed not in one office but in two or three. Even the vital administration of personnel matters was thus divided. Certain personnel functions were performed in a section of the chief clerk's office. Others were performed in the office of the superintendent of buildings and grounds. The consequence was that the Library lacked the administrative supervision and staff to develop a considered personnel policy. It had no grievance procedure, no announced policies covering promotions and the posting of vacancies, no announced policy with reference to Library unions or staff relations, and no such systematic re-examination of Library classifications as is necessary to the maintenance of salary levels under the classification system.

It was in large part, therefore, the effort of a single Librarian and chief assistant librarian to deal with masses of forms, vouchers, pay rolls, and the like which led to a study of the possibilities of reorganization. But there were other and more substantial reasons as well. After my appointment was confirmed by the Senate but before I took office, I was earnestly approached by a number of librarians of university and other libraries who begged me to "do something" about the delay in the delivery of Library of Congress cards to purchasers. I was therefore aware, before I came to Washington, that something was wrong at some point in our cataloging and card-selling operations; and I appointed, shortly after I took office, a co-ordinating committee on processing to look into the whole operation and report to me. The committee was made up of the chief cataloger, the chiefs of the accessions, card, and classification divisions, the director of the union catalog, the chief of the co-operative cataloging service, and the chief assistant librarian. All the various complaints, criticisms, and charges which had reached me from librarians and others in various parts of the country were sent along to the committee for consideration—complaints that the output per cataloger was down by one-half since the beginning of the century, charges that filing into the public catalog was months in arrears, criticisms that the catalogers were untrained, etc. The committee wisely called in the doctors and the specialists. It heard Miss Mann, Professor Harriet MacPherson, Mr. Metcalf, Mr. Gjelsness, Mr. Trotier, and Mr. Wright. And, when it reported on December 9, 1939, it announced findings which suggested that something had to be done and done promptly. There was, said the committee, an unprocessed arrearage in the Library of 1,670,161 volumes — that is to say, better than a million and a half of the six million volumes and pamphlets (exclusive of maps, music, manuscripts, prints, etc.) estimated to be held by the Library of Congress at that time were not represented in the public catalog. And, what was worse, the arrearage was piling up at the rate of thirty thousand books and pamphlets a year.

A similar, though less spectacular, report was made to me at about the same time on the subject of acquisitions. I had been struck, as anyone, I think, would have been, by the piles of book order cards which provided the perennial backstop on Martin Roberts' desk. I had been impressed also by the complaints of that devoted and insatiable book purchaser, the late law librarian, John Vance. Mr. Vance had told me, with courtesy but firmness, that he was continually losing books he wanted to buy because the purchase forms backed up in the chief assistant librarian's office. When I questioned the chief assistant librarian, he admitted the charge but contended that it was necessary for him to examine every title proposed for purchase, whether he knew anything about the book or not: somebody had to do it.

Since Martin Roberts worked twelve to fourteen hours a day in any case and since he would have had to work eighteen or twenty to pass on all book orders, it seemed to me clear that something was wrong with the administration of the purchasing system and perhaps with the system itself. I therefore asked all chiefs of divisions and consultants (issuing my first general order for the purpose) to tell me what steps they habitually took to inform themselves of the books the Library should have and of the books it could secure. Their replies made it obvious that the Library had no considered acquisitions program but depended rather on the activity of sellers in offering materials than on its own activity as a buyer in deciding what materials it needed and seeking them out. I therefore appointed a committee of those members of the Library's staff principally concerned with purchases and asked them to consider what the existing situation was, what acquisitions policy the Library should adopt, and how such a policy should be administered. This committee, called the "committee on acquisitions policy," listened to specialists and experts from outside the Library, such as Dr. Leland, Dr. Raney, Dr. Zook, Dr. Adams, Dr. Swingle, Dr. Blachly, Mr. Metcalf, and others, and duly made its report. Of its recommendations on acquisitions policy I shall speak below. What is immediately relevant here is the indication given by its report that reorganization might be necessary in the acquisitions procedures as well as in the processing procedures and the administrative practices. The committee informed me that, of forty important subjects listed for study,

> twelve receive relatively adequate attention from heads and other members of divisions, consultants, librarians, and other agents; thirteen of the forty subjects are partially and inadequately provided for; and in fifteen, or over one-third of the forty subjects, no general provision is made for the initiation of orders. Thus it appears that general philosophy, American and United States history, the social sciences and law generally, music, fine arts, oriental languages and literature, medical disciplines come in the first group; religions, classical archaeology, geology, classical and modern European languages and literature, the mathematical and physical sciences and agriculture fall in the second group; while general history, special national histories, modern fields of anthropology, the whole subject of education, the earth and biological sciences, medical arts and specialties (provided for, indeed, in the Army

Medical Library) and technology come under the group for which there is no regular and adequate provision as to recommendations.

A closely related—an inevitably related—situation was found to exist in the reference work of the Library—in both the reference work for Congress and the reference work for the Government as a whole and for the general public. The legislative reference service was inadequately staffed to perform the duties the Library owed Congress, and the general reference staff was inadequate to the demands made upon it. A certain number of special divisions with subject specialists, some of them of the first competence, had been created; but they had been created rather as opportunity offered than as the service demanded. General reference inquiries in fields in which special divisions had not been established were referred to the reading rooms staff; and the reading rooms staff, though an able staff and certainly one of the most obliging in the world, was not a faculty of scholars nor could it offer first-rate scholarly guidance in all the fields not covered elsewhere.

Moreover, the combination of reference functions, book-service functions, and custodial functions in the same man or group of men was neither efficient nor, however it may have looked on the surface, economical. Every assistant wanted to be a reference man or, in any case, a desk man in the public service; and the custodial responsibilities languished. There had been a count of materials "by estimate only" in 1898 and a "new count of printed books and manuscripts" in 1902. Thereafter there had been a single inventory of the classified collections which began in 1928 (June) and ended in 1934 (May), showing 170,692 volumes missing from their places. (Of these, materials represented by 91,359 entries had been found by 1941; and by spring, 1944, materials represented by an additional 24,990 entries had been located, reducing the entries for missing books to 54,343.) No officer of the Library in a position to make his voice heard was charged with primary custodial responsibilities; the various special divisions had their own, often conflicting, procedures for book care and binding; and a tremendous arrearage of some 373,721 volumes requiring binding and unfit to be used until they could be bound had accumulated.

It was the attempt to deal with these various factual situations rather than an a priori decision to reorganize the Library of Congress which led to the changes of 1939–44. And the changes, in consequence, were not blueprint changes conceived in advance but administrative adaptations. The first step was obviously to secure the funds necessary for an attack upon the most urgent problems. The subcommittee on the legislative bill of the House committee on appropriations has generously agreed to let me file supplemental estimates three months after the date when estimates are properly due, and I was thus given a brief period to study the Library's situation and to submit a statement of its most pressing needs as I then saw them.

It is hardly necessary to say that the document in which this statement was presented was something less than a complete account of the requirements of the Library of Congress. It did, however, attack the principal problems as they then appeared—the failure of the processing operations to keep up with acquisitions, the lack of subject specialists in numerous fields of legislative and general reference, the inadequacy of funds for book purchase, the shockingly low Library salaries, the lack of administrative officers and administrative controls, etc. Special emphasis was put on the alarming situation in the processing operations where eighty-two additional positions were requested; on the need for first-class reference assistants in the legislative reference service, where ten additional positions of this character plus some twenty other positions were estimated as necessary; on the lack of subject specialists to cover the "orphan" fields of acquisitions and reference work, where the Library had no present coverage and where eleven places were wanted; on the appropriation for book purchase, where an additional $275,000 was requested; and on Library salaries, where $108,720 was requested for within-grade promotions while awaiting reclassification. Altogether, an increase of the appropriation from $3,107,707 to $4,189,228 was asked.

The subcommittee considered these estimates with the care and understanding it has demonstrated throughout the five years in which I have been privileged to deal with it. And these words, I may add, are not put here as a formality or a mere politeness. They come from the heart. The subcommittee as I have known it under the Honorable Emmet O'Neal of Kentucky and the Honorable Louis Rabaut of Michigan has demonstrated again and again its devotion to the Library of Congress and the things for which the Library stands. It has not always given us the things we wanted most, and it has never given us everything we wanted; but its decisions have been just, and its care for the present and for the future of the great Library for which its appropriations provide has been as evident as its judgment and good sense.

The results of my first appearance before the committee were as mixed as they have been since. After a careful two-day hearing the committee recommended, and the Congress allowed, a total increase of $367,591 in the appropriation for the Library. Fifty new positions in the processing divisions, together with the position of co-ordinator of these divisions, were allowed. A $30,000 addition was made to the book purchase fund, and various other increases were voted; but the reference specialists in the general and the legislative reference services were not allowed, nor the position of assistant librarian in charge of acquisitions and the scholarly services. For increases in Library salaries we were instructed to request reclassification by the Civil Service Commission.

The most important gain was, of course, the fifty new positions in the processing divisions and the new position of co-ordinator. It was essential that the best use be made of these positions; and though I was, and am, grateful for the work of the Library's co-ordinating committee on processing, I felt it desirable to have a completely objective and disinterested study made by highly competent members of the profession not connected with the Library's staff. Funds were made available by the late Frederick Keppel, president of the Carnegie Corporation of New York, whose warm and imaginative support of the Library during his lifetime was a continuing source of strength and confidence to me, as to so many others who remember him with gratitude and affection. And on April 10, 1940, a committee, which came to be known as the "Librarian's Committee," was set up. Its chairman was Prof. (now Dean) Carleton B. Joeckel, of the University of Chicago Graduate Library School; and the members, in addition to the chairman, were Mr. Paul North Rice, of the New York Public Library, and Dr. Andrew D. Osborn, of the Harvard College Library.

The report of this committee is undoubtedly one of the most important documents in the history of the Library of Congress. Submitted, because of its character, as a confidential paper, it has been regarded as confidential ever since.

The committee's principal recommendations were

naturally devoted to the reorganization of the Library's processing operations, but it did not confine itself to that field. It also proposed, following the earlier *Statement of the Librarian of Congress in Support of the Supplemental Estimates*, that book selection and reference services be combined under an assistant librarian; and it indorsed the proposal of the Library's committee on acquisitions policy that a systematic book budget be set up with quotas and allotments to the various subject areas – though it did not take up the difficult policy question of *which* subject areas and *what* quotas. On this point the committee contented itself with the suggestion – often made outside Washington but rarely in it[1] – that the co-ordination of the activities of the two hundred and fifty Federal libraries might produce substantial savings.

As regards processing, the committee's proposal was that an "acquisition and preparation" department be set up under an assistant librarian to combine accessioning, cataloging, classification, card sales, and the union catalog.

The accessions division was planned as the purchasing and receiving agency for all books, pamphlets, serials, and other materials acquired by the Library, except copyright material and current newspapers. Its suggested units were: order section, gift section, serial record section, and a duplicate and exchange section.

[1]Two notable exceptions are the Army Medical Library and the library of the Department of Agriculture, with both of which the Library of Congress has worked out co-operative and collaborative procedures of great and increasing value. Colonel Jones and Mr. Shaw, having great libraries of their own, realize that the last thing a library of the size of the Library of Congress wants to do is to "take over" anything – it has troubles enough as it is. They are therefore free of the fear of being engulfed which effectively keeps many of the other Federal libraries from even entertaining the notion of collaboration with the Library of Congress.

The catalog and classification division, in the proposed plan, was to be a merger of the separate catalog and classification divisions. The new division would take over the functions of descriptive cataloging, assignment of subject headings, classification, labeling, and mechanical preparation of material for the shelves. On the basis of function the following sections were recommended: descriptive cataloging, subject heading and classification, and processing. The latter section was to include the clerical and subprofessional activities of the new division—temporary cataloging, shelflisting, card preparation, etc. In certain instances the functional principle was to be carried over into the organization of subsections, including a searching subsection in the processing section and a co-operative cataloging subsection in the descriptive cataloging section.

The card division was to be continued, with the general function of supplying printed cards to other libraries, its work to be confined to its primary function as a sales and distributing agency. It was not to attempt to serve as a supplementary cataloging division or as a book-selection agency. The proposed reorganization of the card division called for five sections: administration, accounting, searching, card drawing, and stock.

Finally, because the technical operations of the union catalog resembled those of the catalog and classification division, it was recommended that the union catalog be incorporated in the acquisitions and preparation department.

These specific recommendations were combined with a number of comments on existing operations which should be briefly mentioned. The committee was impressed by the difficulties of administration in the processing divisions. The great complexity of the Library machine had prevented effective control of technical operations and had permitted great variations in the quantity, quality, and uniformity of work done in the various divisions and sections. It had been impossible to maintain qualitative standards of performance because of the enormous increase in accessions. The quality of administration had also declined to such a degree that administrators had been unable or unwilling to find solutions for the resulting difficulties. More responsible administration, more careful planning of the work program, and more systematic methods of informing and instructing the staff regarding their duties and assignments were needed. The committee recommended the preparation of a manual showing the general framework of Library organization, together with a series of divisional and sectional manuals showing the detailed procedures followed in the various sections.

The committee's report also emphasized the deficiencies in statistics of current additions to the Library as well as of total holdings and the failure of the administrators to establish individual records of work performance in the processing divisions. It was recommended that statistics be revised and standardized and that individual work records be used as tools of administration wherever possible.

In the absence of statistical data the committee guessed that the costs of the technical processes in the Library were extremely high and probably out of line with comparable costs in other large libraries. A new tradition of efficiency and speed in processing activities was recommended as a prime requisite if the Library was to achieve more efficient operations at reduced costs.

It was suggested that the card division review its sales program in terms of the present distribution of card sales and possible extensions of the present system to a larger number of subscribers. The division of accessions, the committee felt, should also review its practices in purchasing books and periodicals in order to determine whether more favorable discount rates might be secured. A strong effort should be made to reduce the high costs of printing and binding, and there must be recognition of the need for modifications in the form and fulness of cataloging. Finally, a highly competent professional personnel must be developed. The recruiting policy for the professional positions should be radically changed, and clerical and professional duties should be more accurately defined.

It will be evident from this abstract of its comments and recommendations that the Librarian's Committee did not undertake to present a blueprint for reorganization but rather a critique accompanied by suggestions. Since the critique was extensive and the suggestions were numerous, I submitted the report to selected members of the staff for comment before attempting to make up my own mind as to the action to be taken. One step, however, was so clearly indicated—was, indeed, so urgently necessary—that I decided to take it at once and without waiting for the reactions of my colleagues to the report as a whole. Some kind of departmental organization was essential if the Library was to function at all. The committee had repeated again and again its finding that administrative controls were weak in the Library as a whole, as well as within the Library's divisions; and the reason, as the committee saw it and as the Bureau of the Budget had seen it before, was also the reason as I saw it: a lack of upper administrative staff.

I therefore issued, at the end of June, 1940, two general orders (Nos. 962 and 964) setting up an Administrative Department and a Reference Department. Mr. L. Quincy Mumford, generously loaned to us by the New York Public Library for the purpose, was appointed co-ordinator of the processing divisions on July 2, 1940, to take office on September 1 (General Order No. 970); and on September 18, 1940, after my colleagues had reported their reactions to the committee's report, the Processing Department was established by General Order No. 981. Since no "department directors" existed in the Library, with the exception of the new co-ordinator of processing, it was necessary to find the administrators of the new units by assigning men from other jobs.

The director of the Administrative Department was found by assigning to that position Mr. Verner W. Clapp, the administrative assistant to the Librarian, whose position, in turn, had been found by reviving the position of executive assistant, which had preceded the position of chief clerk. The director of the Reference Department was found, after various essays, by assigning Dr. Luther H. Evans, who had become chief assistant librarian following the death of that devoted and selfless public servant, Mr. Martin Roberts. The result was to deprive the Librarian of the assistance of his general executive officer, giving him, instead, officers in charge of the Library's three principal operations. It was not an ideal arrangement, but it was an improvement. And it worked more or less satisfactorily for three years, until the chief assistant librarian was able to return to his post, leaving the administration of the Reference Department to the former reference librarian and superintendent of the reading rooms, Mr. David C. Mearns.

As far as the basic structural framework of the Library of Congress is concerned, its "reorganization" was the division into departments of the "Library proper" to complete the departmentalization begun by the statutory establishment of the Copyright Office and the Law Library. Following the issuance of General Orders Nos. 962, 964, 970, and 981, the Library of Congress consisted of five departments: Administrative, Reference, Processing, Law Library, and Copyright Office. One change has been made in this structure since. At the end of the fiscal year 1943 the Administrative Department was liquidated, its units being transferred to the office of the chief assistant librarian, and an Acquisitions Department was created out of the units of the Reference Department and Processing Department engaged in acquisitions work (General Order No. 1188, June 30, 1943).

But, though the basic change was simple, the related changes were sometimes complicated and can only be understood by an examination in some detail of the evolution of the three new departments within themselves. Since the most extensive changes were made in the processing operations, it will be convenient to begin there.

The processing department

As originally established by General Order No. 981 of September 18, 1940, the Processing Department consisted of five divisions, rather than the four recommended by the Librarian's Committee, but did not include the union catalog as the committee had hoped it would. Included were the accessions, card, catalog preparation and maintenance, descriptive cataloging, and subject cataloging divisions. The chief difference between the committee's recommendation and the general order was that divisional status was given by the general order to three units which the committee had proposed to treat as sections—descriptive cataloging, subject heading and classification, and "processing" (i.e., temporary cataloging, shelflisting, card preparation, etc.).

General Order No. 981, however, was a preliminary order only. It was followed on December 23, 1940, by General Order No. 1004, which established departmental organization in greater detail. The principal provisions were these:

The accessions division continued as the purchasing and receiving agency for books, pamphlets, and other materials acquired by the Library. It received gifts, transfers, and deposits, arranged exchanges, approved invoices and vouchers for payments, and kept financial records of book expenditures and incumbrances.

The card division continued to supply printed cards to other libraries. Its principal function became that of a sales and distributing agency.

The subject cataloging division was to perform all functions involving the subject analysis of books — namely, classification, assignment of subject headings, and the shelflisting of materials added to the classified collections. It was to

> classify books and pamphlets according to the Library's own classification, and assign subject headings to them; assign author or other book numbers to them and record them in the shelflist; classify them according to the Decimal Classification; and, for the time being, maintain an alphabetical record of serial publications.

The division included the following sections: subject cataloging, shelflisting and serial records, and decimal classification.

The descriptive cataloging division was responsible for the establishment of author and title entries and the descriptive cataloging of all materials cataloged in the Processing Department. Its work was described as including the preparation of copy for all entries, except subject entries, established in the Processing Department (music, manuscripts, maps, and Orientalia were cataloged in the special divisions); the editing of copy supplied by other libraries which cooperate in cataloging; and correspondence with libraries and individuals inquiring as to principles and practices of cataloging.

The division consisted of the following sections: general catalog, copyright, short form, documents, periodicals, society publications, law, editions and reprint, co-operative cataloging, and proof.

The catalog preparation and maintenance division was to centralize the clerical and subprofessional work of the cataloging processes and to relieve the professional workers of those duties. It included certain subprofessional duties formerly carried on in the accessions and card divisions. The following work was assigned to the division: sorting gift material; searching orders, gifts, and exchanges; temporary cataloging; card preparation; filing and maintaining the library catalogs, including the process file; correcting and adding to catalog cards; labeling, perforating, and bookplating; mimeographing of catalog cards; and general messenger work.

The division included these sections: searching, temporary cataloging, card preparation, filing, duplicates and additions, and labeling.

In sum, the new department as originally set up brought together under central administrative control all operations necessary to prepare newly acquired materials for the shelves with these exceptions: the accessioning of periodicals and newspapers (handled in the periodicals division of the Reference Department); the accessioning of Government documents acquired by exchange (handled in the documents division of the Reference Department); the accessioning of certain other materials received directly in the Reference Department; the cataloging of newspapers, maps, prints, music, manuscripts, and materials in oriental languages (cataloged, if at all, in the special reference divisions); and the preparation of materials for binding (handled in the Reference Department).

General Order No. 1004 was the constitution and charter of the Processing Department down to October 27, 1942, when it was superseded by a new general order (No. 1163) designed to tighten the organization and to make certain changes dictated by the experience of the department's first two years. In the interim three operations had been added to those covered by General Order No. 981. A process file had been established in the catalog preparation and maintenance division in October 1940, to assist in locating books in process and to enable the searchers of recommended orders to satisfy themselves that the book recommended had not recently been received by gift, exchange, or otherwise. A central serial record had been set up in the accessions division in August 1941. And a duplicate and exchange section had been created in the accessions division on November 15, 1941, which became the general exchange section on May 11, 1942, when the division took over responsibility for the accessioning of Government publications coming in by exchange, deposit, or gift. In addition, Mr. Mumford's leave of absence had expired and Mr. Herman H. Henkle, director of the School of Library Science at Simmons College in Boston, had become the first permanent director of the department, his appointment dating from January 26, 1942.

General Order No. 1163 made several important changes in the sectional organization of the department's divisions, designed (1) to draw related functions more closely together in the sectional organization; (2) to reduce the number of sections to more manageable proportions; (3) to increase the field of activity of certain sections to make possible greater flexibility of work assignment within the sections; (4) to concentrate responsibility for technical supervision in the descriptive and subject cataloging divisions by designation in each division of the position of principal cataloger; and (5) to expand the Processing Department office to provide for the maintenance of personnel records, work records, and cost-analysis records on a departmental basis.

In the accessions division the Hispanic, law, and general order sections were united as units of the newly constituted order section; and the general exchange, documents exchange, and gift sections were united as units of the exchange and gift section.

The serial record was expanded to absorb some of the serial recording functions of the shelflisting and serial records section in the subject cataloging division, becoming the serial record section of the accessions division.

In the catalog preparation and maintenance division the purchase searching, gift searching, preliminary cataloging, and process information units were united to form the book section. The card preparation and filing sections were united with the proof-reading section from the descriptive cataloging division to form the card section. The labeling unit was transferred from the division, plating and perforating of new accessions being placed in the purchase accessioning unit of the accessions division. Plating and perforating of newly bound serials and labeling of all classified books were transferred to the shelflisting section of the subject cataloging division.

The assistant chief of the descriptive cataloging division became the principal cataloger and deputy chief of the division, and the assistant chief of the subject cataloging division became the principal cataloger and deputy chief of that division—a change designed to concentrate responsibility for technical supervision of the work in each division. General review of card copy for style was assigned to a new officer, the editor of card copy, with the transfer of the proofreading section to the catalog preparation and maintenance division. The copyright and general sections were abolished and the work redistributed to the newly established English language section and foreign language section. The law and documents sections were modified to become the American and British law and documents section and the foreign law and documents section, with the work of the former sections distributed accordingly.

In the subject cataloging division the serial record unit was abolished, its work being divided between the shelflisting section in the same division and the serial record section in the accessions division.

In the card division the card drawing and the stock and supply sections were combined to form a card stock and drawing section.

Finally, the staff of the Processing Department office, which had previously consisted of director, administrative assistant, and director's secretary, was expanded and reorganized to provide for the maintenance of personnel, work records, and cost accounting on a departmental basis.

A department secretary was added, and four clerical positions were transferred to the department office from the divisions.

These changes completed the design of the Processing Department as we see that design. One major and two minor modifications have been made in the department since, and there are still processing operations in the Reference Department which we hope some day to put where they belong, but no further alteration in the basic structure is contemplated.

The minor modifications were the transfer from the Reference Department to the Processing Department of the binding office (binding in our practice is a processing operation or a custodial operation, depending on whose book is being bound) and of the union catalog, which is also a processing or a reference operation, depending on which end of the cat you pick up first.

The major alteration was the establishment of the Acquisitions Department, referred to above. Experience convinced us that both the *Statement of the Librarian of Congress in Support of the Supplemental Estimates* and the *Report of the Librarian's Committee* were wrong in recommending that the book-selection part of book purchasing should be combined with reference work and separated from book accessioning. It was clear that the people who recommended books for purchase would necessarily be reference specialists and therefore members of the Reference Department. It was clear also that the business of purchase would always be a specialized business requiring specialized personnel. But we were convinced that the Library would never receive the books it should receive until all book-selecting *operations* were centralized in one administrative unit under one administrative head. We therefore set up the Acquisitions Department on July 1, 1943, and transferred to it the units of both Processing and Reference primarily engaged in book selection and purchase. This meant that the accessions division transferred its loyalties from the Processing Department to the Acquisitions Department and that the catalog preparation and maintenance division of the Processing Department having lost its searching unit to the Acquisitions Department, was abolished, its preliminary cataloging section going to the descriptive cataloging division, its proof, card preparation, and filing units to the card division, and its process information unit to the Processing Department office.

It may be helpful, by way of recapitulation, to let

Mr. Henkle describe the present organization of his department in his own words:

The descriptive cataloging division is responsible for preparing preliminary catalog entries for all titles directed to the Processing Department and for preparing copy for the printer of the book descriptions which constitute the content of the Library of Congress printed cards, exclusive of the designation of subject headings and classification numbers. "Descriptive cataloging," in the range of the division's responsibilities, involves the establishing of authors' names to be used officially in the Library's catalogs; the recording of the titles and other bibliographical characteristics as well as physical descriptions of the books cataloged; the editing of the catalog copy for the printer; and the continuing correction and change of existing catalog entries as called for in connection with the cataloging of new acquisitions. The division also carries primary responsibility for the program of cooperative cataloging.

The division consists of seven sections: preliminary cataloging, English language, foreign language, American and British law and documents, foreign law and documents, serials, and co-operative cataloging.

The preliminary cataloging section is the point at which new acquisitions normally enter the Processing Department from the Acquisitions Department. The section is a key control point in the processing operations, being responsible for preparing the initial mastercard which, as it proceeds through the cataloging divisions, becomes the printer's copy for Library of Congress printed cards, and also carrying responsibility for distributing items to be cataloged to the several sections of the division.

The division is administered by a chief, who has an administrative assistant and a secretary; a principal cataloger, who also serves as deputy chief of the division; an editor of card copy; and the section heads. The division has a staff of ninety-one members.

The subject cataloging division is the successor of the

former classification division, and it inherited responsibility for subject headings from the former catalog division. This new division has, accordingly, full responsibility for the analysis and record of the subject content of the Library's collections as it is recorded in the public catalog. Intimately involved in the functions of this division, too, is the very important responsibility for continued review of the published classification schedules and list of subject headings, in the light of growth and change in all fields of knowledge.

Also within the "subject cataloging" functions of the division is the classification of books by the decimal classification system, as a service to other libraries. The division has responsibility, also, for shelflisting all classified titles and for performing certain of the terminal steps in preparation, namely, labeling all classified volumes and plating and marking volumes which are bound after being received by the Library.

The subject cataloging division consists of three sections: subject cataloging, decimal classification, and shelflisting. The division is administered by a chief, with a secretary; a principal cataloger, who also serves as deputy chief of the division and directs the work of the subject cataloging section; an editor of subject headings; an editor of classification; and the heads of the decimal classification and shelflisting sections. The staff of the division numbers fifty-six members.

The card division is primarily responsible for superintending arrangements for printing catalog cards, for maintaining the stock of cards, and for distribution of Library of Congress printed cards through sales to other libraries. Additional functions assigned to the division are proofreading the galley proof for printed cards, preparing the cards, when printed, for use in the Library's catalogs, and filing printed cards in the public and official catalogs and preliminary cards in the process file.

The division consists of nine sections: catalog investigation; searching; revising; documents; series order; subject order; card stock and drawing; proofreading, card preparation, and filing; and the secretary's office, which includes the accounting unit. The division is administered by a chief, with a special assistant and the staff of the secretary's office, an assistant chief, and the heads of the sections. The staff of the division numbers one hundred and fifty-seven, with occasional additional assistants employed on an hourly basis.

The union catalog division exists primarily to serve American libraries and research institutions by developing the union catalog of the holdings of the co-operating libraries and by serving as a central clearing house for locating books anywhere in the United States. The union catalog is the principal source of information for interlibrary loans.

No change has been made in the organization of the division; but under appropriations made available by Congress the staff has been greatly expanded for the purpose of carrying forward one-, two-, and five-year projects of the expansion of the catalog. The normal staff of fourteen members was increased for the year 1943-44 to thirty-nine. The division is administered by a chief, with a secretary, and an assistant chief.

The binding office serves as the clearing house for all materials bound after receipt for addition to the collections. It maintains and clears records of all material routed to the bindery by custodial divisions, itself preparing most of the unbound monographs. It has final responsibility for reviewing all materials prepared for binding and particularly for making arrangement of materials accord with the catalog records.

The office has a staff of seven members and is administered by the binding officer and an assistant binding officer.

The department office of the processing department serves as the co-ordinating unit of the department for personnel, budgetary, production, and cost-accounting records (except that cost accounting for card distribution is performed in the secretary's office of the card division) and supplies information about books in process. The office is under the immediate supervision of an administrative assistant to the director, with a staff of seven assistants.

The procedures involved in the preparation of books

for the collections, from the preparation of preliminary cards through the filing of printed cards in the catalogs and the labeling of books for the shelves, are procedures which require close co-ordination. The primary purpose of the department organization is to provide this co-ordination, together with the direction necessary to efficient operation, the responsibility for which rests with the director. He is assisted by an assistant director, a technical assistant, and a secretary. The technical assistant conducts and directs research on the technical problems of the department. To aid him and to assist the director and the Librarian in estimating the department's work and its needs, statistical data are being accumulated as rapidly as possible. Cost-accounting procedures, established with the aid of the general accounting office, have been in operation for card distribution for about two years. As a result of these accounting records, the Library is enabled to conduct its card sales on a more business-like basis and to determine card prices which are equitable both to subscribing libraries and to the Government of the United States. Until recently, however, the Library has not had precise knowledge of the cost of its other processing operations. Again with the aid of the general accounting office, a continuing system of work records and cost accounting has been set up for the descriptive and subject cataloging divisions and will be extended shortly throughout all operations of the department. It is anticipated that a report of the system will be made available when possible to other libraries.

The acquisitions department

Although the creation of a separate Acquisitions Department came late in the process of reorganization, consideration of the problem came early. It came, in fact, at the beginning. My first general order, as I have noted above, was issued to learn what the Library's book-selection practices were; and the committee on acquisitions policy, which was to report on the entire problem, was appointed a month after I took office. There has never been a time in the past five years when the question of acquisitions was not under consideration in its policy or its administrative aspects. It is still under study today; and, without doubt, it always will be. There is no final answer to the question of what books the Library of Congress should secure, nor is there any final answer to the question of how best to secure them. All we have done – all we have tried to do – has been to hammer out working answers which provide a basis for present operations. Our "Canons of Selection" are certainly not eternal statements of objectives, but at least they are statements of objectives which will stand; which will shape and orient our acquisitions programs until better statements take their place. And our acquisitions procedures, though they are far from perfect, are at least stated procedures which take into account the various elements of the administrative problem as we know those elements.

The Library of Congress, in other words, has not learned in the last five years how the collections of a national library can be made and kept as complete as they ought to be. It has not even learned how complete the collections of a national library, in a nation of other great libraries, ought to be. But it has faced both questions. It has tried to find answers. And – what is more important – it has tried to find those answers for itself. The Library of Congress no longer waits for dealers to offer books, or for collectors to give them, or for publishers to deposit them for copyright. The Library of Congress now takes active and affirmative steps of its own, and on its own account, to find out what it lacks and to secure what it needs. Reorganization of our acquisitions activities, whatever else it means or does not mean, means that.

And it began on that issue. The questions submitted to the committee on acquisitions policy[2] in November 1939, were these: (1) Whether the Library of Congress should attempt to formulate a policy of accessions based upon a knowledge of present deficiencies and a plan for their correction by purchase or whether it should depend upon offers of sale of collections, offers from the book trade, from collectors, and from donors, etc.; (2) whether a policy of accessions should be based upon the assumption that the Library of Congress should be as nearly complete as possible, or upon the assumption that it should specialize in fields where it is now strong, leaving other fields to other libraries, or upon the assumption that the Library should be "well rounded"; (3) whether the operation of a plan of acquisitions should be directed by the accessions division; whether the accessions division or the division of bibliography or some other officer or unit should formulate a want-list; and whether such a list should be made the basis of standing orders.

The committee's report, filed on December 19, 1939, found, as I have noted above, that under the then existing practice of the Library of Congress no provision was made for initiating orders in fifteen of forty important subject fields and that inadequate provision was made in thirteen others, leaving only

[2]The members of the committee were: Dr. Sioussat, chief of the division of manuscripts, chairman; Dr. Bentley, consultant in philosophy; Mr. Childs, chief of the division of documents; Dr. Clark, consultant in economics; Dr. Hanke, director of the Hispanic foundation; Mr. Mearns, superintendent of the reading rooms; Mr. Vance, law librarian; Dr. Zahm, chief of the division of acronautics; Miss Dennis, assistant chief of the division of accessions; and Miss Hellman, chief of the division of bibliography.

twelve which received "relatively adequate attention." To correct this situation the committee recommended:

1. The creation of a centralized agency in the Library for the co-ordination of all requests and recommendations for purchase, through the establishment of an acquisitions office under a director who would be advised by staff members broadly informed of the needs of the Library's collections:

2. A flexible book budget whereby a minimum sum might be counted upon for purchases in each field of acquisitions;

3. Stricter enforcement of the copyright act to insure deposits of copyrighted books;

4. The designation of agents of the Library in foreign countries to insure the procurement of essential foreign books;

5. An increase in the number of consultants and other advisers in special subject fields;

6. Closer co-operation between the Library and the academic and learned world, e.g., through the establishment of joint committees representing the learned societies and the staff of the Library and through the establishment of fellowships for scholars whose work might be directed in the interest of the Library; and

7. The institution of surveys of those parts of the Library's collections which had been neglected because no separate divisions or special consultants had been assigned to supervise their custody or growth.

On the policy question of "completeness" of the collections the committee concluded that "completeness" was desirable in the following fields: (1) Law and government, including governmental publications, (2) the civilization of the Americas, and other fields which may be described as national interests; and (3) all that contributes to information about books, with respect to the Library's catalogs and to bibliography in the widest significance of that term.

As regards the relation of the acquisitions policy of the Library of Congress to the acquisitions policies of other libraries—federal and nonfederal—the committee reported: First, that the Library might well rely on the Army Medical Library and the library of the Department of Agriculture to cover their respective fields, aiding them in building up their collections rather than attempting to duplicate those collections; second, that the Library could not safely rely on the collections of other federal libraries to cover special fields; third, that the Library should not attempt to build up collections in special fields in which it was not strong and in which other libraries in the United States were known to be strong; fourth, that the Library should, however, maintain strong collections of its own in a condition of strength regardless of holdings elsewhere; fifth, that gifts of distinguished special collections should not be refused regardless of holdings elsewhere; and, sixth, that the Library of Congress should recognize a special duty to secure foreign materials not readily available to smaller libraries.

In terms of appropriations for increase of the collections, this meant, in the committee's opinion, $500,000 a year for Increase General instead of the then appropriation of $118,000. The committee estimated that it would cost $200,000 a year to buy important foreign publications in the fields of the Library's interest. The balance was thought necessary for the purchase of noncopyrighted American materials, extra copies, and older materials of all origins.

Since the Library was falling behind at the estimated rate of 30,000 volumes a year in processing the materials secured under its $118,000 appropriation for increase, I did not feel justified in accepting the committee's figures; nor did I think it would be possible, in view of the outbreak of war, to buy $200,000 worth of books a year in Europe. We did, however, request in our supplemental estimates for the fiscal year 1941 an added $100,000 for Orientalia, an added $75,000 for Hispanic material, and $100,000 for purchases and photocopying in Europe. Thirty thousand dollars of this estimate was granted, raising the appropriation for Increase General to $148,000. But our efforts to provide for the "orphan" subject fields were, as I have noted, unsuccessful. The subcommittee on the legislative bill was sympathetic but firm.

Unlike the processing problem, the acquisitions problem had to be attacked without new positions beyond those made available in the accessions division for purchase routines. The attack to be made was, however, clear. The Librarian's Committee reinforced the findings and conclusions of the committee on acquisitions policy on most points and emphasized the need for action. Its recommendations were:

1. That the reference services of the Library be united in a Reference Department, with an assistant librarian in charge; and that this assistant librarian, in addition to having responsibility for directing, supervising, and co-ordinating the work of the reference service divisions, be also the principal book-selection officer, with responsibility for controlling and co-ordinating the book-selection work of the Library. "Book selection," said the committee, "is a joint process, participated in by chiefs of divisions and others; but final decisions are made by the Assistant Librarian, and all suggestions for purchase are referred to him."

2. That a systematic book budget, under the control of the assistant librarian in charge of the Reference Department, be set up, with quotas for the various divisions and careful consideration of the proper distribution of funds among the various fields of knowledge.

3. That the accessions division serve not as a book-selection agency but as a purchasing and receiving agency for all materials acquired by the Library and as

the agency to execute orders received from the book-selection officers; and that it assume responsibility for maintaining in a central serial record a consolidated account of all serials received by the Library, the recording of which was currently maintained, so far as it was maintained at all, in a number of divisions.

4. That the assistant librarian in charge of reference, or his delegate, or delegates of the assistant librarians in charge of reference and processing, select material for the collections from current copyright receipts.

5. That the Library initiate a vigorous policy of encouraging gifts; that the gift section of the accessions division be enlarged; but that the Library feel free to reject inappropriate gifts.

6. That possibilities be explored for co-ordinating the activities of the Library with those of other Federal libraries in the District of Columbia with a view to making substantial savings through the elimination of duplication of collections. A Federal library council for this and similar purposes was recommended.

Partly for reasons of logic and partly for practical reasons, we began not with the specific recommendations of the Librarian's Committee but with the underlying question of policy. The practical reasons related to the reclassification of Library positions by the Civil Service Commission. Commissioner Arthur Flemming, to whose warm interest and humane intelligence the Library of Congress owes a debt I am proud to acknowledge, had suggested that a consideration of the Library's objectives by the Library's staff would be helpful not only to the commission's investigators but to the Library itself. Meetings were, therefore, held with the Library's principal officers in the summer of 1940, and the Library's functions and objectives were discussed. They were not, I should note, the most successful meetings I can recall. One or two of the more articulate of my elder colleagues approached the discussion in the spirit of the senior benches at a faculty meeting:

Change was undesirable and any discussion which might lead to change was in doubtful taste. The Library of Congress was too big and too old—above all, too old—to ask itself what it was doing and why and for what purpose.

Once faced, however, the seriousness and urgency of the central question demanded an honest and serious answer, and drafts of objectives for the Library's service and for the selection of its materials were prepared and circulated and finally approved. These "Canons of Selection" define the Library's objectives with reference to three categories of users: first, Members of the Congress; second, officers of the Federal Government and the staffs of the various Government departments and agencies, including the Supreme Court and its bar; and, third, the general public. Because it is impossible for the Library of Congress to "collect everything," selection of material must be made on the basis of the anticipated needs of these three classes of users in the order given. The "Canons of Selection" apply to the Library's acquisition of material by purchase, but not to its acquisition by gift or by deposit for copyright. Their text follows:

1. *The Library of Congress should possess in some useful form all bibliothecal materials necessary to the Congress and to the officers of government of the United States in the performance of their duties.*

To this Canon only one exception is made. A large number of special libraries have been established in the various departments, bureaus, and offices of Government as, for example, the Department of Agriculture, the Office of the Surgeon General of the Army, etc. Where the collections of these libraries adequately cover particular fields in which the Library of Congress is not strong, the Library of Congress will not purchase extensively in these fields but will limit itself to the principal reference works, using its best efforts to strengthen the collections already established elsewhere. Where, however, the collections of the Library are already exceptionally strong they will be maintained regardless of holdings in other libraries. The Reference Department of the Library of Congress will make it its business to know the extent of the collections of these special libraries and will establish, with the librarians in charge, machinery for cooperation both in the maintenance of these collections and in their use.

2. *The Library of Congress should possess all books and other materials (whether in original or copy) which express and record the life and achievements of the people of the United States.*

To this Canon there is one obvious exception. Where official records of the Federal Government are deposited in the National Archives the Library will secure only such copies as are necessary for the convenience of its readers. It will, however, attempt to secure all printed documents, Federal, State, and municipal.

Again the Library's principal concern here is with national rather than local records, and though it recognizes that many so-called local records are, or many become, of national significance (as, for example, local histories of which it has a distinguished collection) the emphasis of its effort is upon records of national interest, and its primary concern as regards local manuscript records is to stimulate their collection in appropriate localities.

3. *The Library of Congress should possess, in some useful form, the material parts of the records of other societies, past and present, and should accumulate, in original or in copy, full and representative collections of the written records of those societies and peoples whose experience is of most immediate concern to the people of the United States.*

Two exceptions to the third Canon should be noted. First, the Library of Congress as the central United States depository for the publications of all foreign governments will attempt to secure all the *official* publications of all governments of the world. Second, where, aside from such official documents, other American libraries, whose collections are made broadly available, have already accumulated, or are in process of accumulating, outstanding collections in well-defined areas, in which areas the Library of Congress is not strong, the Library of Congress will satisfy itself with general reference materials and will not attempt to establish intensive collections.

The "Canons of Selection" provided the outlines of a basic policy of book selection. Their application in practice, however, presented problems. Since new appropriations for this purpose had not been voted, we were obliged to do what we could with the means available. Consequently, provision was made in the establishment of the new Reference Department in June, 1940, for the centralization there of book-selection responsibilities; and, in particular, responsibility for the approval of books for purchase devolved upon the reference librarian who was then Mr. David C. Mearns.

A first step was the preparation of a schedule of allotments, by subject fields, from the appropriation for the increase of the collections. Sums in varying amounts were set aside for the development of each class of material, the sum allotted being determined by considerations of known deficiencies in the collections, expected acquisitions from sources other than purchase, the extent of literary production in the field, and the relative importance of the subject to the Library in accordance with the "Canons of Selection." This schedule of allotments covered all subjects in which the Library was interested except law. The appropriations for the increase of the Law Library and for books for the Supreme Court were left, for the time being, to be expended by the law librarian and the marshal of the Supreme Court, under the direction of the Chief Justice.

Allotments having been set up, it became necessary to find recommending officers for each field.

This was done in part with the aid of a grant from the Carnegie Corporation for the establishment of fellowships in the Library of Congress and in part by the appointment of associate fellows from the Library staff and from other government departments. The Carnegie grant, now unfortunately discontinued by the corporation, was, in my opinion, one of the most hopeful and helpful efforts thus far made to bridge the gulf between libraries and the scholars who use them. The purpose was to prepare a certain number of young scholars every year to make scholarship serviceable to libraries in order that libraries might be as serviceable as they should be to scholarship. The corporation, as Mr. Keppel stated in announcing the grant, acted from a conviction "that American cultural institutions can be greatly strengthened if scholars will accept a responsibility for the holdings of the national library and if the national library will accept a responsibility for the instruction of scholars in the services it is prepared to render." I cannot too strongly emphasize my conviction that the withdrawal of the Carnegie grant at a time when the Library's fellowships had clearly demonstrated their usefulness, not only to the Library of Congress but to national scholarship, was a tragic loss to both.

The first five fellows of the Library of Congress and their fields were: Dr. Richard H. Heindel, University of Pennsylvania (modern European history); Dr. Edward P. Hutchinson, Harvard University (population); Dr. Jerrold Orne, University of Minnesota (romance languages and library science); Dr. William E. Powers, Northwestern University (geology); and Mr. Francis J. Whitfield, Harvard University (Slavic languages and literatures). During the academic year 1941–42 the fellows included: Dr. Byron A. Soule (chemistry), Mr. Manuel Sanchez (technology), Dr. Waldo Chamberlin (naval history), and Dr. Benjamin A. Botkin (folklore); during the academic year 1942–43: Dr. E. Franklin Frazier (American Negro studies) and Dr. Sidney Kramer (war bibliography). The present holders of fellowships are: Dr. Edward Mead Earle (military science), Dr. Walter Livingston Wright, Jr. (Near Eastern studies), Katherine Anne Porter (regional American literature) and Dr. John Kozák (Czechoslovakian studies). The fellowship of Mr. John Peale Bishop (comparative literature) was interrupted by his ill health, which has since tragically terminated in his death.

By the summer of 1942 these various changes in acquisitions policy and practice had shaken down to such a point that a definite statement could issue. General Order No. 1151, of August 25, 1942, strengthened the control exercised by the reference librarian over the selection of materials, extending it to acquisitions by every means – gift, deposit, and exchange, as well as purchase. Expenditures from the appropriations for the law collections were alone excepted. The commission for the selection of copyright deposits was abolished, its duties being shared by the reference librarian and the director of the Processing Department. These officers were also to examine and select materials from receipts by gift, transfer, and exchange. The responsibility of the accessions division was also clarified: The division was to be the sole office of record for incoming materials.

But, if the organization and procedures were clear, they were far from satisfactory. The reference librarian could not act as the principal book-selecting officer of the Library without injury to his work as reference librarian – and vice versa. Moreover, the lack of administrative connection between book selection (in the Reference Department) and book buying (in the Processing Department) was a weakness which became daily more obvious. The result was the decision, debated through the winter of 1942–43 and finally taken in the summer of 1943 (June 30), to remove final responsibility for book selection from the Reference Department and to put it in the hands of an officer responsible for acquiring the material selected. This meant a new Acquisitions Department, which was set up by General Order No. 1188.

In effect, this order centers in the new department all acquisition activities. Recommending officers, though they may perform duties in other departments—usually the Reference Department—report, in their work of recommendation, to the director of the Acquisitions Department; and all receiving and accessioning work is done in the department's divisions. The accessions division was transferred to the new department from the Processing Department. The functions of the old documents division with respect to the acquisitions of Government documents were transferred to the exchange and gift division. (Accessioning functions had previously been transferred from the documents division to the accessions division.) Selection of material from unsolicited receipts (copyright deposits, gifts, and exchanges) was centered in the department, as was allotment of purchase funds, Law as well as General. Purchase and accession searching, formerly functions of the catalog preparation and maintenance division, were transferred to the order and to the exchange and gift divisions, respectively. In addition, the serial record was transferred from the Processing Department and set up as a division.

Altogether, the new department is made up of a director and his office (eleven employees), two assistant directors for planning and operations, and three divisions—order, exchange and gift, and serial record—the work of which is described by the director, Mr. Clapp, as follows:

The order division (thirty-one employees) has sole responsibility for acquisitions where the expenditure of money is involved, for purchase searching, and for pricing. The exchange and gift division (twenty-eight employees) is responsible for the acquisition of material by gift, exchange (including the international exchange of government publications under the Brussels Convention and other treaty engagements), various provisions of law, and official donation, and for the recording of conditional deposits and intramural transfers of materials. This division is responsible also for bookplating and marking of material received bound, for accession searching, and for the preparation and issuance of the *Monthly Checklist of State Publications*. To the serial record division (nineteen employees) are sent all serials from whatever source (except nongovernmental daily newspapers) for accessioning record. Besides this original accession record, however, the serial record maintains the basic and permanent record of the Library's holdings of serials, bound and unbound, processed and unprocessed; it enters cataloging and classification indicia into bound volumes, and its records have displaced the shelflist entries for this type of material; it keeps the control record of decisions affecting the selection, retention, distribution, and processing of serial publications throughout the Library.

The establishment of the new department coincided with the adoption of a new method of reporting important acquisitions. Prior to 1940 important new acquisitions were listed in the annual report in the chapters then written by the chiefs of the various special divisions. The result was, first, that materials not the responsibility of any particular special division were frequently overlooked; second, that materials were announced many months, and often as much as a year, after acquisition. But, in any case, the *Annual Report of the Librarian of Congress* was not, and should not be, a book-lover's intelligencer. It has too many statistics to report and too many personnel changes to list. We therefore decided in the summer of 1943 to report on new acquisitions in a supplement to the annual report which would be published quarterly. The Public Printer approved the plan as easing somewhat the autumnal strain on his presses. Allen Tate, our distinguished consultant in English poetry, agreed to take on the editorial task; and the first issue of the *Library of Congress Quarterly Journal of Current Acquisitions* appeared in November 1943. Its reception has convinced us that a publication such as we had in mind and Mr. Tate has realized can serve American scholarship.

The reference department

The creation of the Reference Department differed from the creation of the Acquisitions Department and the Processing Department in that the Acquisitions and Processing departments were constructed by affirmative action whereas the Reference Department evolved. There was, it is true, a general order (No. 964, of June 29, 1940) at the beginning of the history of the Reference Department; but it did little more than pile up some twenty heterogeneous divisions, accumulated by the Library over the course of haphazard time, and direct the then director of the legislative reference service, Dr. Evans, and the then superintendent of the reading rooms, Mr. Mearns, to make a department of them. The functions to be performed by the new department were, it is true, named: reference, book selection, book service, and the care and custody of books on the shelves. The divisions were named also. They were the reading rooms division (the main reading room, the annex reading rooms, the study room service, the social sciences reference room, the local history and genealogy reading room, the reading room for the blind, and a proposed science and technology reading room), the documents division, the legislative reference service, the periodicals division, the rare book collection, the manuscripts division, the Orientalia division, the Semitic division, the Slavic division, the Smithsonian division, the aeronautics division, the project books for the adult blind, the Hispanic foundation, the fine arts division, the music division, the maps division, the union catalog, the photoduplication service, the consultants, and "any consultant services or scholarly services which might be set up, such as the projected fellowships of the Library of Congress."

Messrs. Evans and Mearns were told, moreover, what results they were expected to accomplish. In reader service and the care and custody of books they were to centralize the Library's operations, permitting only such exceptions as they could not avoid. To help them in this labor they were given two new officers: a keeper of the collections, charged with responsibility for the physical custody, security, and preservation of the Library's collections (Alvin W. Kremer) and a chief of the book service (Robert C. Gooch).

In reference work and book service they were told that the new department should (1) assign responsibility for reference work and book selecting in the various fields of knowledge to those officers of the Library and members of the Library staff having competence in the particular fields. (In fields in which no officer possessed particular competence, interested members of the staff were to be encouraged to participate in the work of selection and reference); (2) establish a system of routing of reference problems to the persons to whom responsibility for the various fields had been assigned; (3) establish a system for the initiation of recommendations of book purchases by the members of the Library staff responsible for the various fields of knowledge; (4) assure the systematic examination of publications, book reviews, and special articles in the various fields, with a view to the prompt origination of recommendations for purchase of new books in these fields: and (5) provide means by which the collections might be analyzed with a view to building want-lists and developing a rational and affirmative policy of book acquisition.

But beyond these sailing directions and this small crew they were given very little help by the Librarian. What had happened in effect was that all units of the Library not engaged in processing work (Processing Department), in housekeeping functions (Administrative Department), in copyright work, or in law were set off together and called a department. The excessive "span of control" which had made the Librarian's life burdensome was transferred in large part to the new "director" — who, moreover, did not exist, since the position requested had not been granted by Congress. Moreover, one of the divisions transferred was the vast (for the Library of Congress) and sprawling (for any library) reading rooms division, which combined in one organ-within-the-organism such disparate functions as book service, book custody, circulation within and without the Library, and reference work both high and low.

It is not remarkable that the Reference Department which resulted was a department in name only and that its substantial creation was obliged to wait for almost four years. Dr. Evans and Mr. Mearns struggled manfully. The chief assistant librarianship, with Dr. Evans in it, was thrown into the hopper. The position of reference librarian, with Mr. Mearns in occupancy, was added as a second in command—but with book selection to handle as well. The keeper of the collections and the chief of the book service labored endless hours. The large, diffused, and various staff performed its large, diffused, and various duties. But, though much of the greatest importance was accomplished, a department, conscious of itself as a department and working functionally as a department, was not evolved. General reference policies were imposed upon the heterogeneous divisions making up the department, and reference reports were brought into conformity with those policies. Administrative channels which had not previously existed were established and administrative relationships set up. But, because the new department did not reflect function in its organization, a functional organism was not created; and it soon became apparent that nothing but a complete reconsideration and a new start would be effective.

Whether or not the new start could have been made sooner than it was is extremely doubtful. For one thing, the solution of the processing tangle demanded and received priority of treatment not only in the appropriations committee but in the minds of the Library administration. The situation discovered there was manifestly dangerous and could not be allowed to continue. A second circumstance operating to delay a thoroughgoing reorganization of the Reference Department was the war. I have not wished to emphasize the fact in this report, but readers will have noticed that the entire reorganization of which I am writing took place after the outbreak of the war in Europe, and most of it during our participation in the war. The effect of the war on the Library was the effect familiar elsewhere: Manpower was lacking, and service demands, though they decreased in number, increased in difficulty. Moreover, the Librarian was drafted for other services for better than a year and from time to time thereafter. Whether my absence as director of O.F.F., as assistant director of O.W.I., and as organizer of O.W.I.'s London branch was an advantage or a disadvantage to the Library of Congress in its general operations may well be a matter for debate. In terms of the Library's reorganization, granted that reorganization was necessary, it could only be a retarding factor, since reorganization was necessarily my responsibility and could not go on without me.

These, however, are excuses. They do not dispose of the fact that the real reorganization of the Library's vital reference services was delayed to the winter of 1943–44 and General Order No. 1218 of March 25, 1944. Prior to that date, however–in the fall of 1940, to be exact–the "Canons of Service" had been worked out in Library conferences, with the result that the reorganization, when it came, had a philosophy to go on. Since the philosophy of library service is somewhat less clear than Kant, it may be worth while to brief the reasoning by which we arrived at our conclusions.

At the beginning of our discussion two views were advanced–or perhaps it would be fairer to say that participants in the discussion were urgently invited to have views with reference to two opposed positions: One, that a library is a kind of machine to drop a book into a reader's hand, the machine having no further responsibility or, indeed, interest– except to get the book back; the other, that a library is a group of human beings who accept a responsibility to make any part of the printed record available to society, by whatever means is most intelligible and most effective, the responsibility ending not with the mechanical delivery of a book but with the identification and production of the text or the information needed.

As between these two positions, there seemed, at first, to be unanimous agreement on the part of my associates that the second was the more nearly correct. Indeed, some of them went so far as to suggest that the first definition was the old definition of a library and that the second was the more modern. But there was no disagreement that the second was applicable to the Library of Congress.

Proceeding from this point, an attempt was made to discover what the precise obligations of a library of the second category were: Particularly, what was meant by the statement that a library accepts a responsibility to "make available" pertinent parts of the total record. As an extreme position, it was suggested that a library, such as the Library of Congress, might accept an obligation to publish by radio, by print, by near-print, or by other means, those materials, of fact and of opinion, which, in its best judgment, bore upon the controversial issues which a democratic nation faces. Would it be possible for the Library of Congress to publish material of this kind in a form useful to the electorate? It was generally agreed that such a program would require an amount of time and a number of advisers beyond the capacities of the Library.

A more moderate conception of library responsibility was next discussed. It was suggested that the Library of Congress might fulfil its obligations by preparing annotated bibliographies and other briefs of the record for publication in newspapers or by other agencies wishing to use them – the Library of Congress accepting responsibility for its selection of authorities and for its presentation of the historical record. It was pointed out that the Library has a duty always to present both sides of controversial problems.

Here there seemed to be a keen sense of the difficulties involved, and retreat was suggested to a still more moderate position – the position ascribed to another great national library – i.e., a limitation of the responsibility of the Library to the assistance of accredited and qualified scholars who might work in the Library for scholarly purposes. As to this, however, there was general agreement that the Library of Congress could not fulfil its responsibility in so narrow a manner. First, it was pointed out that the Library would be limiting its reference assistance to those who need such assistance least. Second, it was pointed out that such assistance to scholars in the production of scholarly works to be read by other scholars would not result in the publication of the essential record to the people at the time when the people most had need of it.

At this point it became necessary to review our first decision as to the two concepts of a library. A medial position was suggested: that the principal responsibility of a library is to deliver a book into the hands of the man who asks for it but, at the same time, to undertake what were referred to as "extra-curricular" services to certain types of readers, chosen on some basis not defined. As to this, it was replied that there might be a considerable difference between the notion that a library's responsibilities end with the delivery of books, reference services being "extra-curricular" adjuncts, and the alternative notion that a library's real and essential function is the activity which is sometimes referred to as "reference work," the serving-out of books being merely incidental to that function.

Gradually the definition sharpened. It was recognized, as a matter of course, that the primary obligation of the Library of Congress was owed to Congress and that its second obligation was the service of officers of government charged with the conduct of official business. The obligation to the Nation as a whole, however, proved more difficult to define.

In an effort to resolve that problem and to define the areas of agreement, I tried my hand at a draft of

"Canons of Service" which was circulated for comment on September 11, 1940, and which we included, in corrected form, in the annual report for that fiscal year. The canons do not answer the dark and cloudy questions discussed during the summer — questions which wiser men with more time to devote will, I hope, consider at greater length. They do not define the word "library" in service terms. They helped, however, to orient the department which was to follow four years later, and they are therefore given in full:

1. *The Library of Congress undertakes for Members of the Congress any and all research and reference projects bearing upon the Library's collections and required by Members in connection with the performance of their legislative duties.*

There are no exceptions to this rule so far as the Library's conception of its obligations is concerned. Only a lack of means to provide the necessary, and necessarily skilled, staff will justify a failure on the Library's part to meet all such demands.

2. *The Library of Congress undertakes for officers and departments of government research projects, appropriate to the Library, which can be executed by reference to its collections, and which the staffs of offices and departments are unable to execute.*

These projects are deferred, except in case of emergency, to reference projects undertaken for Members of the Congress.

The rules establishing the Library's reference and research obligations to Members of the Congress and officers of government suggest, in turn, its reference obligations to other libraries and to the public in general. As in the case of its collections, the reference facilities of the Library are facilities created for the use of Members of the Congress, etc., as representatives of the people and are therefore the facilities of the people. For this reason, but subject to the priorities established by the greater urgency of the research needs of Members of the Congress and officers of Government, the reference facilities of the Library are available, within appropriate limitations, to members of the public acting either through universities or learned societies or other libraries or directly. The "pool of scholarship" which the Library of Congress is obliged to maintain in order to perform its obligations to the Congress and to the government is, in other words, as much the property of the people as its collection of books. These facts determine the third rule defining the reference objectives of the Library.

3. *The reference staff and facilities of the Library of Congress are available to members of the public, universities, learned societies and other libraries requiring service which the Library staff is equipped to give and which can be given without interference with services to the Congress and other agencies of the Federal Government.*

This policy is active as well as passive. Passively considered it means that reference inquiries, and requests for bibliothecal service, which cannot be satisfied by other libraries or scholarly institutions nearer the inquirer, may be submitted to the Library of Congress which will respond to them within necessary limitations of time and labor. Actively considered, the Library's policy in this regard means that the Library of Congress, as the reference library of the people, holds itself charged with a duty to provide information to the people with regard to the materials they possess in its collections, and with an obligation to make its technical and scholarly services as broadly useful to the people as it can.

The reorganization of 1944 was carried forward on the basis of these canons. It was accomplished only after full discussion and the greatest possible opportunity for criticism and comment. Work began in the department in the fall of 1943, and a preliminary outline was distributed to the professional staff before the December 1, 1943, meeting of the professional forum. A series of discussions was also held with division chiefs, and the daily meetings of the

Librarian's Conference were devoted to the project from time to time over many months.

Broadly speaking, the purpose in view was to take the department down and reconstruct it in terms of its principal functions: (1) custody, (2) circulation, and (3) reference, transferring its book-selection duties to the new Department of Acquisitions, which had been set up to receive them. This meant the dissolution of the reading rooms division—a reform long overdue. It meant the unification of custodial responsibilities, previously scattered among the reading rooms and the special divisions, and the reaffirmation of "the classic organization" of the collections which the general order defined as having been intended "to make available, in and through a single classified collection, all material which can be so organized and serviced, separate collections being maintained only when the nature of the material (e.g., manuscripts) or the character of the alphabet (e.g., Chinese) makes the maintenance of a separate collection unavoidable." It meant a custodial and delivery service, a loan service, and a reference service adapted not only to the various categories of reference demands (congressional and other) but to the realities of reference inquiries (informational and scholarly).

The organization which resulted and its relation to the organization which went before can best be understood by comparing the pre-reorganization chart (I) with the post-reorganization chart (II); see pages 152 and 154. Here, as in the case of the other departments, I shall let the director, Mr. Mearns, describe the organization and operation of his department in detail:

> *The legislative reference service.* —Only a brief account of the legislative reference service is necessary. The service existed prior to the March reorganization and did not undergo any drastic change at that time. Its

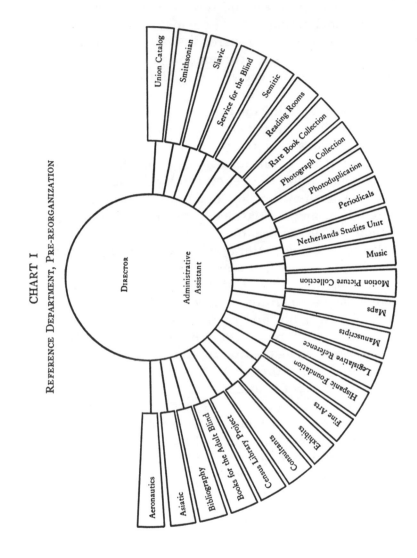

CHART I

REFERENCE DEPARTMENT, PRE-REORGANIZATION

DIRECTOR

Administrative Assistant

Union Catalog
Smithsonian
Slavic
Service for the Blind
Semitic
Reading Rooms
Rare Book Collection
Photograph Collection
Photoduplication
Periodicals
Netherlands Studies Unit
Music
Motion Picture Collection
Maps
Manuscripts
Legislative Reference
Hispanic Foundation
Fine Arts
Exhibits
Consultants
Census Library Project
Books for the Adult Blind
Bibliography
Asiatic
Aeronautics

internal responsibilities and scope and its relationship to the other services were more carefully defined. It had been apparent that, previous to the reorganization, the legislative reference service was not a division of the Reference Department in the same sense as were, for example, the rare books division or the aeronautics division. The legislative reference service (sixty-eight employees) supplies an overall reference service to Members of Congress, with particular emphasis on subjects related to proposed or pending legislation. In the reorganization this fact became decisive, and the legislative reference service was set up as a service parallel with the public reference service. To be sure, the Library as a whole has compelling obligations to perform reference service for Members of Congress, but where such work is done elsewhere the legislative reference service coordinates it for congressional use.

The legislative reference service retains charge of the congressional reading room and in so doing assembles, charges, and loans materials requested by Members of Congress or their families. It forwards such charges to the loan division, which has over-all responsibility for maintenance of records of loans. Under the reorganization the legislative reference service will continue to compile and publish indexes to federal and state laws, digests of public general bills, and basic data studies on matters of legislative concern.

The circulation service. —From the standpoint of administrative units, the circulation service represents the most drastic departure from the previous organization. The custodial and circulation services it performs were the scattered responsibility of the former reading rooms division, including the government publications reading room and many of the special divisions. The previous unintegrated divisional structure of the Reference Department and the relative autonomy of the divisions had resulted in unintegrated and unrelated collections. Books were issued and loaned from a dozen different divisions, and there was no centralized responsibility for records of books in use within the Library or of outside loans. In terms of service to readers, this situa-

CHART II

REFERENCE DEPARTMENT, ORGANIZATION, MARCH, 1944

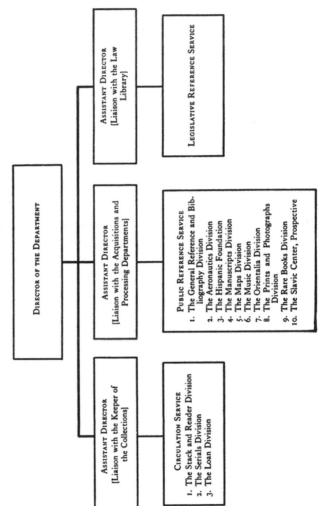

DIRECTOR OF THE DEPARTMENT

ASSISTANT DIRECTOR
[Liaison with the Law Library]

LEGISLATIVE REFERENCE SERVICE

ASSISTANT DIRECTOR
[Liaison with the Acquisitions and Processing Departments]

PUBLIC REFERENCE SERVICE
1. The General Reference and Bibliography Division
2. The Aeronautics Division
3. The Hispanic Foundation
4. The Manuscripts Division
5. The Maps Division
6. The Music Division
7. The Orientalia Division
8. The Prints and Photographs Division
9. The Rare Books Division
10. The Slavic Center, Prospective

ASSISTANT DIRECTOR
[Liaison with the Keeper of the Collections]

CIRCULATION SERVICE
1. The Stack and Reader Division
2. The Serials Division
3. The Loan Division

tion was reflected in a regrettably high precentage of failures to supply desired books either from the central desk in the main reading room or from the special divisions; and the reverse side of this picture was an interference with reference service by the custodial responsibilities of the reading room and the special divisions.

The separation of custodial and circulation responsibilities from reference duties does not imply any demeaning of the former. Rather, by providing a hierarchy of custodial positions and duties, it establishes custodianship as a definite professional function of librarianship. In their reaction against the tradition of European librarianship, American libraries have tended to exalt their reference functions and undervalue their custodial functions. In this country the public library movement created and made self-conscious the profession of librarianship, and in great public libraries particularly the problems of custody are apt to receive scant attention. But in the Library of Congress, and, no doubt, in other large research libraries with Nation-wide demands on their resources, the custody and circulation of materials becomes a major operation. These materials include not only books in the millions but also more millions of periodicals, bound and unbound, pamphlets, manuscripts, prints, photographs, maps, sheet music, slides, etc. It is hoped that one of the products of the creation of the circulation service will be a corps of professional curators, trained in the custody and administration of the Library's collections.

The circulation service is made up of three newly established divisions: the stack and reader division, the serials division, and the loan division.

The stack and reader division (eighty employees) issues and delivers material as requested for use in the general reading rooms, divisional reading rooms, and study rooms and for the official use of members of the staff in the divisional offices; it collects and reshelves such materials; and maintains records of materials in its custody and of materials issued and returned. It provides study rooms or other special research facilities in accordance with established policies and passes upon applications for the privilege of access to the book stacks.

The division also has custody of the general classified collections and administers the circulation of materials from these collections to readers and investigators. It maintains, in accordance with standards of custodial care established by the keeper of the collections and approved by the Librarian, the physical and orderly arrangement of materials in the book stacks and in the reference collections in the general reading rooms, selecting deteriorated materials for rebinding and repair. A few collections remain in the custody of special divisions, but the trend is definitely and encouragingly toward centralization. Collections of books formerly in the custody of the aeronautics division, the maps division, the fine arts division, the Slavic division, and the Smithsonian division are now administered by the stack and reader division. Materials such as maps, prints and photographs, sound recordings, etc., which cannot conveniently be integrated with the general collections, by reason of their form, remain in the custody of the respective divisions concerned with them.

Some idea of the scope of the operations of the stack and reader division may be obtained from the following statement concerning the transfer of positions and personnel. From the reading rooms division there were transferred to the stack and reader division the stack inspectors, the stack attendants, the control room attendants, the book distributors, the guards and guides, the personnel of the study room reference service (with certain specified exceptions), the central charge file, the assistant in charge of document collections in the main reading room gallery, two clerks, and twelve messengers. The stack attendant formerly in charge of the collections of the Smithsonian division was also transferred to the stack and reader division.

The serials division (forty-five employees) has custody of certain groups of materials which require, or for reasons of convenience are given, reader and reference service prior to their addition to the general classified collections. Insofar as their custody is not allocated to one of the several special divisions, the following groups are included: periodicals, newspapers, pamphlets, Government documents, books in parts, and ephemera of various sorts. Such materials represent custodial, circulation, and reference problems in all libraries; but in the Library of Congress the problems are magnified by the sheer bulk of the material. With respect to such materials, the functional division as between custody and circulation, on the one hand, and reference service, on the other, has been deliberately set aside. The serials division maintains a reference service in special reading rooms with respect to periodicals, Government documents, and newspapers in its custody; but this service is (with the specific exception of documents) subordinate to its custodial responsibility, which constitutes its primary function.

Because the preponderance of official documents are serials and because their treatment and service as current publications are, to a large extent, comparable with the treatment and service of other kinds of periodicals, the Government publications reading room, its collections, and its staff have been transferred from the reading rooms to the serials division.

The loan division (fifty employees), as its name implies, administers all outside loans (including loans of books, periodicals, maps, music, prints, embossed books, sound recordings, etc.) It should be noticed that the principle of centralization of administrative responsibility has been carried further with respect to outside loans than with respect to the custody or issue of books within the Library. The Library of Congress is a national library, and officers of Government, as well as scholars, confident of its resources, come to it or write to it for reference assistance. A book on loan is not available for use, and in wartime instant availability assumes heightened importance. The practice of individual and inter-library loan has advantages which justify the inconvenience it sometimes occasions, but this inconvenience should be minimized and can be minimized only through a centrally administered loan service maintaining consolidated loan records.

The public reference service.—The public reference service is made up of the general reference and bibliography division and nine other divisions differentiated from one another in terms of subject and regional specialization or in terms of the type of material in association with which their respective activities are carried on. Before proceeding to a description of each division in turn, a brief account can be given of the common activities which bring them together in the public reference service. Public reference divisions exist to provide a reference service to readers in the Library and, through correspondence, outside the Library; they maintain special indexes and reference catalogs; they compile bibliographies and guides to the collections; and their chiefs function as recommending officers in the fields of knowledge reflected by their specialization.

Certain of the divisions, in addition to their reference functions, administer special collections of material not suitable for inclusion in the general classified collections of books. The manuscripts division, for example, has custody of the general collections of manuscripts, transcripts of manuscripts, and photographic reproductions of manuscripts. It catalogs and classifies such material and makes it available for use in a reading room which it administers. The maps division, the Orientalia division, and the prints and photographs division have identical responsibilities for the types of materials with which they are concerned. The rare books division is responsible for the custody and service of those copies of books which, because of their importance to the history of ideas, or their contribution to the progress of literature, or their provenience, or their association with great men and great events, or their monetary value, or their condition, require special facilities for their preservation and supervised use. The music division maintains custody not only of sheet music and sound recordings but of the literature of music as well. Standardized cataloging and classification techniques have been developed to a point which assures the integration of the diverse materials comprising the collection and which obviates the necessity of custodial separation on the basis of form. Moreover, so much of the literature of music contains the only versions of the music itself that it would be practically and administratively impossible to distinguish between the two categories.

The general reference and bibliography division was created by combining the former division of bibliography with the reference personnel and functions of the former reading rooms division — a change first suggested in early 1940 in the *Statement of the Librarian of Congress in Support of the Supplemental Estimates.* As now constituted, the general reference and bibliography division (fifty employees) is organized to respond to all public reference requests which do not require the attention of the special divisions, whether such requests are received in person, by telephone, or by mail.

All consultants and special projects, which formerly functioned under the immediate supervision of the director of the department, are now administratively assigned to the general reference and bibliography division. This provides a means of relating individual or temporary special activities to the general and sustained reference work of the Library.

The relation between specialized and general service in this instance is analogous to the relation between specialists in medicine and the general practitioner. The general practitioner does not treat disease in general but rather those specific diseases which do not fall within one or another of the specialties or which fall within several of them. Further, the knowledge and skill of the competent general practitioner is such that he can treat the average case of many diseases which do fall within the specialties; in most such cases it would be foolish and extravagant to employ the time and talent of a specialist.

No library, no matter how rich and favored, can hope to provide a staff of specialists to cover the whole field of knowledge. Nor can the interests and problems of readers be divided into neat compartments without overlapping or remainder. Current developments are apt to have little regard for yesterday's academic specializations. For example, the learned world in America is divided and organized on the basis of subject specialization. In the present emergency the nation has discovered that it needs not only subject specialists but area specialists as well. Methods of training regional specialists have had to be improvised. The regional bibliographies prepared by nonspecialists in the general reference and bibliography division have contributed something to that training.

The effect of the reorganization on the special divisions is to free them for their proper work. The aeronautics division (five employees) has been relieved of its former custodial responsibilities and encouraged to undertake a more elaborate bibliographical program in connection with the Nation-wide reference service it renders. The Hispanic foundation (eight employees), relieved of custody of its materials and separated from its archive of Hispanic culture, which, as a photograph collection, becomes a part of the prints and photographs division, is free for its proper reference function of developing and co-ordinating the Hispanic activities of the Library and fostering cultural interchange with Hispanic nations. The foundation will continue to prepare special bibliographies, guides, indexes, and other publications appropriate to its service.

The manuscripts division (seventeen employees) has not been changed internally by the reorganization. However, its newly established position within the public reference service serves to define more precisely its primary functions in the field of American civilization.

The maps division (nine employees) is responsible for the custody and service of the collections of maps and atlases. The books formerly in the custody of this division have been transferred to the general collections in the custody of the stack and reader division. As in the case of aeronautics, the maps division, relieved of part of its custodial responsibility, is free to develop an extensive reference service in the fields of geography and cartography.

The music division (sixteen employees), like the manuscripts division, remains essentially unchanged in the reorganization. It is relieved, however, of the task of maintaining a loan service of its materials.

The Orientalia division (fourteen employees), formerly the Asiatic division, is responsible for the custody and service of all materials written or printed in oriental languages (including Chinese, Japanese, Semitic, Arabic, Persian, Turkish, etc.). The former Semitic division has been made a section of the Orientalia division. The responsibility of the Hispanic foundation for fostering cultural relations with the Hispanic countries is matched by a similar responsibility which the Orientalia division has of fostering cultural interchange with oriental nations.

The renaming of the prints and photographs division (eleven employees) represents an attempt to indicate the true responsibilities of the former fine arts division with regard to graphic materials in its custody. Books on art in the custody of the former fine arts division have been transferred to the general collections. Because of the importance of prints and photographs in connection with exhibits, the exhibits office has been transferred to the prints and photographs division, and exhibits have been made the special responsibility of an assistant chief of this division. Although this assistant chief becomes, in effect, the executive officer responsible for exhibits, the responsibility for initiating projects for exhibits and assisting in the assembly and preparation of materials continues to be a function of the chiefs of Reference and other divisions.

In addition to custodial responsibility, the rare books division (nine employees) maintains a reference service appropriate to its collections. Most requests for reference service which necessitate the consultation of incunabula, sixteenth-and seventeenth-century publications, American imprints before 1820, the principal editions of important historical, scientific, and literary works, first editions, limited editions, de luxe editions, specially and extra-illustrated editions, fine bindings, unique copies, the literature of the typographic and book arts, and other collections of rare books are directed to it.

The Slavic center soon to be established will be modeled on the Hispanic foundation. It will render reference service in respect to the Library's Slavic collections and will foster cultural interchange with Slavic countries.

There remain several former divisions of the Reference Department which have not been accounted for in the above statement. Of these, the photoduplication service has been transferred to the administrative offices under the direction of the chief assistant librarian. The union catalog has been transferred to the Processing Department, where it obviously belongs; and the service for the blind, being a loan service, has been made a section of the loan division. The fiscal and administrative sections of books for the adult blind have been transferred to the administrative offices under the chief assistant librarian. The former book selection and reference work of this division is now the responsibility of the public reference service. The reference service formerly conducted by the Smithsonian division is now the responsibility of a consultantship in the history of science. As a reflection of our experience in the operation of a science and technology reading room, and responsive to demands upon our collections in those fields, plans for the future anticipate the creation of a science division which will include not only this consultantship but the aeronautics division and other scientific reference services, existing or projected.

A summary of the department's functions and the units by which they are performed was prepared for the use of the Library staff. Since it gives a convenient over-all view of the organization, it is reproduced here.

A. The department maintains custody of—

1. The general collections (exclusive of law, but including Hispanic materials previously in the custody of the Hispanic foundation, the proceedings and transactions of learned societies and academies formerly in the custody of the Smithsonian division; the literature of geography previously in the custody of the division of maps; aeronautical publications previously in the custody of the aeronautics division; Slavic materials previously in the custody of the Slavic division) through } the stack and reader division

2. Manuscripts (including transcripts and photographic reproductions of manuscripts) through } the manuscripts division

3. Rare books (including microfilm reproductions of printed materials) through } the rare books division

4. Prints and photographs through } the prints and photographs division

5. Maps and atlases (including topographic views) through } the maps division

6. Music and the literature of music through } the music division

7. Embossed books and sound books for the blind through } the loan division

8. Current periodicals, documents, pamphlets, and ephemera; and newspapers, current and noncurrent, through } the serials division

9. Orientalia through } the division of Orientalia

10. Microfilms in general through } the microfilm reading room in the rare books division

B. The department processes materials* as follows:

1. Prints and photographs through } the prints and photographs division

2. Manuscripts (including transcripts and photocopies of manuscripts) through } the manuscripts division

3. Maps and atlases through } the maps division

4. Embossed books and talking books for the blind through } the service for the blind section of the loan division

5. Materials in Chinese, Japanese, Indic, and other Eastern languages through } the division of Orientalia

C. The department circulates materials to readers—

1. In the general reading rooms and study rooms through } the stack and reader division

2. In the reading rooms of the special divisions above named through } the special divisions above named and through the microfilm reading room in the rare books division

3. Outside the Library buildings through } the loan division

---

* All processing procedures followed by divisions of the Reference Department are subject to the approval and revision of the rector of the Processing Department.

D. The department gives reference service—

1. To Members of Congress—

   a) In all matters relating to legislation through } the legislative reference service†

   b) In all other matters } See below

2. To investigators and general readers—

   a) In the history and topography of the United States

      i) By manuscripts, transcripts of manuscripts, photoreproductions of manuscripts and similar source materials through } the manuscripts division and the incumbent of the chair of American history

      ii) By pictorial materials illustrative of American life through } the prints and photographs division

      iii) By maps through } the maps division

      iv) By rare printed Americana through } the rare books division

      v) By other printed materials (including local history and genealogy) through } the general reference and bibliography division

   b) In Hispanic history through } the Hispanic foundation

   c) In Far Eastern, Indic, and Near Eastern history through } the division of Orientalia

   d) In Slavic history through } the Slavic center (which is to be created)

   e) In Netherlands history through } the Netherlands studies unit

   f) In history—general, national and local (except the history of the United States)—through } the general reference and bibliography division or one of the special regional units‡

   g) In geography and cartography through } the maps division

   h) In religion and philosophy through } the general reference and bibliography division or one of the special regional units

   i) In political science, economics, and sociology through } the general reference and bibliography division, the serials division (and its government publications section), or one of the special regional units

   j) In population and demography through } the census library project of the general reference and bibliography division

   k) In education through } the general reference and bibliography division, or one of the special regional units

† The legislative reference service is available only to Members of Congress.

‡ The special regional units are: the Hispanic foundation, the Slavic center, the division of Orientalia (consisting of Chinese, Japanese, Indic, and Semitic sections and the provisional Iranian section), and the Netherlands studies unit.

l) In music and the literature of music (including ing American folk song and sound recording) through } the music division

m) In the graphic arts (including fine prints and the literature of the fine arts, together with the iconography and photographic record of the life of the people of the United States) through } the prints and photographs division

n) In literature and linguistics (including fiction) through } the general reference and bibliography division and its consultant in poetry in English, the rare books division, or one of the special regional units

o) In aeronautics through } the aeronautics division

p) In natural sciences through } the general reference and bibliography division and its consultant in the history of science (Jefferson Room)

q) In applied sciences (technology) through } the general reference and bibliography division (Jefferson Room)

r) In military and naval science through } the general reference and bibliography division (Jefferson Room)

s) In bibliography and library science through } the general reference and bibliography division, or any of the special divisions

t) In incunabula, history of printing, private presses, and *editiones principes* through } the rare books division

u) In periodicals and newspapers in general through } the serials division

v) In manuscripts in general through } the manuscripts division

Administrative units

An account of the regrouping and reorganization of the several administrative services and offices of the Library could be made as long as it would inevitably be dull. Since, however, it was the inadequacy of the fiscal services which most impressed outside surveyors of the Library, such as the representatives of the Bureau of the Budget, and since the lack of an adequate personnel office and a considered personnel policy was a continuing annoyance through three years and more, some account of reorganization in this general field is essential. It could be summed up, in terms of the grouping of the units involved, by saying that they were first combined in an Administrative Department (General/Order No. 962 of June 28, 1940) and then transferred, when the Administrative Department disappeared and the chief assistant librarian took over his proper duties as general executive officer, to the office of the chief assistant librarian (General Order No. 1190 of July 5, 1943). But though this summary account would take care of the secretary's office (ten employees), the supply office (four employees), the mail and delivery service (fourteen employees), the office of the superintendent of Library buildings and grounds (two-hundred and eighty-six employees), and the disbursing office (seven employees), none of which were materially altered internally, and though it would also suffice, perhaps, for the photoduplication service (ten employees) and the division of books for the adult blind (twelve employees), both of which were added to the chief assistant librarian's cares when he took over his executive duties, it would not account adequately for changes in the accounts office (six employees) and the personnel office (twenty-two employees). Nor would it cover the publications office (one employee) and the information office (two employees), which had not previously existed.

Of these latter it is enough to say that each performs the duties which would be expected of its name. One handles stocks of Library publications and the like. The other supplies information to the public through the press and otherwise. The new duties of the accounts office and the personnel office must, however, be spelled out at greater length.

Accounts office.—General Order No. 962 supplied an officer the Library had lacked in the past and had badly needed: a budget officer. The administrative assistant as director of the department was to act as budget officer of the Library, supervising the preparation of budget estimates, developing programs of budgeting expenditures, and co-ordinating work within these programs.

To supply the administrative assistant with budgetary information and to impose needed controls on expenditures, a more active and modern accounts office was necessary. It was provided by the same general order. The accounts office was given authority for the maintenance of budgetary control through allotments made by the administrative assistant and was authorized to exercise accounting control over the receipt and expenditure of appropriated, gift, and trust funds and the requisitioning of cash. It was also to examine and to approve for payment all pay rolls and vouchers, to examine the disbursing officer's accounts current prior to the Librarian's approval, and to prepare reports and statistics needed for administrative and budgetary planning.

At the same time, new and modern procedures were worked out for the accounts office with the aid and advice of representatives of the general accounting office. The accounts now maintained by the accounts office comprise a general ledger for appropriated, gift, and trust funds and for the funds of the Library of Congress trust fund board, as well as an allotment ledger for appropriated, gift, and trust funds. Allotments are made by the budget officer to the various departments and divisions of the Library authorized to incur obligations: the Acquisitions Department (formerly the accessions division), the card division, books for the adult blind, the Copyright Office, the mail, music, personnel, photoduplication, publications, and supply offices, and the superintendent of Library buildings and grounds. The accounts office prepares monthly statements for the various divisions reflecting the status of funds under all allotments.

Prior to July 1, 1940, there were a number of divisions of the Library handling collections of moneys. At present there are two: the secretary's office, which receives remittances on account of card sales, sale of photo-duplications, gifts, and miscellaneous transactions, and the Copyright Office, which, in accordance with the act of March 4, 1909, receives and deposits all copyright fees.

Accounts are maintained on an incumbrance basis, and all financial transactions are adjusted to this basis. Only those officers to whom funds are allotted may incur obligations, and then only to the extent of their allotments and subject to other necessary limitations. No account is acceptable for payment unless it appears that a proper statement of the obligation was entered in the books of the accounts office at the time of its incurrence, nor is the disbursing officer authorized to make payment until the account is approved for payment by the accounts officer.

The general effect of these changes has been to separate certifying responsibility from auditing responsibility. Formerly the office of the chief clerk certified accounts and audited its own certifications. Now operating officers certify and the accounts office audits. The new practice has made for sense and simplicity, as well as for safety. Documents are now signed, wherever possible, by officers having personal knowledge of the facts to which they put their names: and the meaningless authentication of forms by officers whose signatures are necessarily mere formalities has disappeared.

Personnel office.—When the chief clerk's office

was abolished in June 1940, and the Administrative Department established, the personnel section of the chief clerk's office became the personnel office of the Library with a director of personnel at its head. It was given responsibility for interviewing applicants and for filing and classifying applications. It was to maintain personnel records, including those formerly maintained in the office of the superintendent of Library buildings and grounds. It was directed to cooperate actively with the Civil Service Commission in classification matters. It was assigned responsibility for the execution of approved personnel policies. It was charged with the duty of hearing grievances and handling appeals from efficiency ratings and decisions as to classification. The Library's emergency room and the nurse were placed under the supervision of its director.

The duties of the office, broadly described in 1940, were more precisely defined by General Order No. 1191 of July 7, 1943, issued when the administrative units of the Library, including personnel, were transferred to the office of the chief assistant librarian. By this latter order the personnel office became responsible, under the direction of the chief assistant librarian, for the full personnel management of the Library, including all matters relating to recruitment, placement, classification, employee relations, grievances, training, health, safety, pay rolls, efficiency ratings. It is responsible not only for the maintenance of central personnel records of leave, retirement, and employee status but also for the study and development of new policies and procedures as they become necessary.

Reorganization in the personnel field was not limited, however, to the administrative organization of the office. It extended to personnel policy as well. Library unions were recognized and encouraged as valuable instruments of good administration. A promotions policy, calling for the posting of vacancies, was worked out in co-operation with Library unions and staff members. A grievance procedure, which has been widely and favorably commented on in the government, was developed in extended conversations in my office between representatives of the unions, representatives of the staff generally, and administrative officers. A staff advisory committee was set up at the suggestion of union representatives and has functioned effectively for two years as a channel for employee proposals and criticisms and as an originator of administrative suggestions of its own. A professional forum meets once a month under the chairmanship of the Librarian in his professional, rather than his official, capacity to hear accounts of Library operations and to discuss the central unsolved problem of a librarian's work – the catalog (or other) control of the constantly increasing mass of printed and near-printed material.

These latter innovations are parts of a general pattern of development which one will approve or disapprove as he approves or disapproves government by discussion. There are those, of course, who disapprove of it – and not all of them live in totalitarian states. Men of certain temperaments find talk annoying – particularly talk in public enterprise. Talk, they say, wastes time. And they are right, of course. But talk, kept within proper limits, can save time also and can gain what time alone might lose. In any event, my colleagues and I – most of my colleagues, at least – believe firmly in government by discussion and believe, further, that experience has justified our belief. We conduct the Library's central administration through the Librarian's Conference, a daily meeting of department heads and principal administrative officers which debates policy decisions and in which principal administrative assignments are made.

Final responsibility for decision is still, of course, the Librarian's, as it must be by law; but conference discussions insure a hearing for all points of administrative view and keep the Library's various officers informed of each other's activities, with the result that administrative interchangeability becomes a practical possibility rather than a paper theory. No officer of the Library of Congress feels that he and he alone can do his job. Others can do and have done it. Mr. Clapp, originally a reference man, ran the Administrative Department for three years and now heads the Acquisitions Department. Dr. Evans, originally head of legislative reference and later head of the Reference Department, is now, as chief assistant librarian, the director of the administrative services previously run by Mr. Clapp. Dr. Hanke, whose principal responsibility as director of the Hispanic foundation has been to foster sound relations with the cultural and learned institutions of the other American Republics, is assistant director of the Reference Department in charge of public reference. Administrative officers of the Library have been warned that they are to move from department to department to insure the Library of Congress against the academic isolationism which has had such harmful effects in American universities and through the universities on American education. I hope they believe the warning was seriously intended.

Government by discussion is not, however, limited to the Librarian's Conference. Both the Processing and Acquisitions departments have committees, under the chairmanship of their directors, on the policies of their operations, the members of which include the principal officers of other units concerned in, or affected by, their work. Bibliographical and other publications are planned by a committee under the chairmanship of Dr. Hanke. And an effort was made before the war — an effort which we hope to renew when the war is over—to plan the relation of the Library of Congress with the learned world and particularly with other libraries through, and with the advice of, a group of scholars, librarians, and lovers of books, whom we have called, in their informally corporate capacity, the "Librarian's Council."

I should like to end a paper, which is already far too long, on this theme. Whatever else our reorganization has accomplished—and I hope and believe it has provided a sensible, orderly, and manageable structure, strong enough to support the great future of which the Library of Congress is so manifestly capable—whatever else the reorganization of the Library has accomplished, it has given, I trust, an increasing number of men and women the sense of participating creatively and responsibly in a work which all of them may well feel proud to share.

If it has done that, I shall feel that my five years as Librarian of Congress, meager as their accomplishment must necessarily seem by comparison with the great decades which went before, were not without their value to an institution I have learned not only to respect but love.

A Slavic
Center for the Library
of Congress · 1944

The changing treatment of Russian books in American libraries has followed the changing pattern of the interest of the American people in the people of Russia. During the years when the Americans thought of the Russians as a remote and different people, Russian books were treated as special collections to be held separately from general library collections and cataloged accordingly. Now that the people of Russia have become a part, and an immediate and present part, of the common world of all peoples, Russian books are being treated not as Russian books but as books.

In the Library of Congress they are in process of incorporation into the Library's general collections, with control through the Library's central catalog. From this time on, the Library's special services in the Russian field will be special services not in terms of the treatment of books but in terms of the relations of men. They will be services, that is to say, intended to bring Russian and American readers together rather than to keep American and Russian books apart.

The incorporation of the Russian collections into the general collections of a library is not without its difficulties. For one thing, the Cyrillic alphabet presents problems for the general staff of any library.

First published in the *American Review on the Soviet Union* 6:11–14 (November 1944).

For another, specialized scholars who have become accustomed to working with Russian materials in separated and isolated collections, regard a different shelving with apprehension, fearing that Russian books will be less available in general collections than they were when shelved alone.

The difficulty of alphabet can, however, be overcome. With the sympathetic assistance of a Congress and an Appropriations Committee which understood the importance, even in time of war, of making Russian materials more readily available, the Library of Congress has now materially increased its staff of Slavic catalogers and has developed a program for the preliminary cataloging of Russian books which will, it is hoped, make broad control of the collection relatively easy.

The apprehension of scholars who have been accustomed to the use of Russian materials in separate collections can also, the Library believes, be met. That apprehension is based in large part upon a misconception as to the uses of systematic classification in a large library. Books systematically shelved under a system of classification, and controlled by a central catalog, are more readily available to a larger public than books shelved in special collections. What is essential now, is to make Russian materials as available as possible to the broadest possible public.

But it is not enough merely to treat Russian books like books and to make them as readily available as other library materials. It is necessary also to supply learned counsel and advice to their users. This purpose the Library of Congress intends to achieve through the establishment of a Slavic Center which will provide American students of the U.S.S.R. with expert assistance and promote the exchange, between the U.S.S.R. and the United States, of librarians and scholars able to interpret the two countries to each other. (Since the principal interest of readers of this magazine is in Russian material, I will confine myself in what follows to our Russian plans, merely remarking in passing that related plans are under development in other Slavic fields.)

The collection, on the basis of which the Library plans to build its services in the Russian field, is a collection of unusual interest to students of Russia as well as to students of libraries, for it is the collection used by Lenin in the late 1890's to complete his *The Development of Capitalism in Russia*. Lenin, exiled in 1897 to Krasnoyarsk, a provincial capital in Siberia, found there a remarkable library of books collected by a merchant of the town named Gennadius Yudin.

Yudin's library, purchased by the Library of Congress in 1907, was reputedly one of the greatest private libraries ever collected. It was extraordinary, not only for its location in an undistinguished town of some 30,000 souls, and not only because its collector was neither a man of wealth nor a man of letters, but because, in spite of these facts, the collection had grown to 80,000 volumes and because it documented with unexpected completeness the flowering of Russian literature in the 19th Century and the history and archeology of Siberia. It included in addition to the usual standard works, solid sets of scholarly publications and journals and rare manuscripts on the Russian discovery and colonization of Alaska.

But great as it was, there were gaps in the Yudin collection — understandable gaps in a Czarist collection but gaps notwithstanding. Writing to his sister on March 27, 1897, Lenin says, "Yesterday I visited the famous local library of Yudin, who welcomed me cordially and showed me his collection. He also gave me permission to work in his library . . ." On the same day, however, in a letter to his mother, Lenin added, "I have found much less material on my subject in the library than one would think in a collection of this size."

The weaknesses of the Yudin collection in 1897 when Lenin used it were still weaknesses in 1907, when the Library of Congress brought the books to the United States in 519 heavy cases. They remain weaknesses today, some forty years after purchase. Great collections, like the Yudin collection, when used as the foundation of library holdings have a natural tendency to determine the form of the structure raised upon them. Although the Library of Congress has added to the Yudin collection since its delivery in Washington, Lenin would still have found our holdings inadequate for the purposes he had in mind, had he turned to them at the end of his life. They are inadequate today in their representation of the new Russia Lenin helped to create.

One of the principal tasks to be undertaken, therefore, before an effective service of Russian materials can be given, is the task of extending the Library's Russian holdings to cover the entire field of Russian publishing activity. This, however, is a problem not in the Library of Congress alone, but in American libraries generally. It can best be solved by cooperative and collaborative effort. With the generous and imaginative assistance of the Rockefeller Foundation, a plan for a collaborative attack on the problem has been worked out and is already in operation.

A group of Russian scholars, under the direction of Professor Karpovich of Harvard, has prepared lists of basic Russian materials in the various disciplines and fields of knowledge to be circulated by the Library of Congress among American libraries specializing in Russian materials. It will be possible to determine by the checking of these lists against existing collections what basic Russian books are now held in American libraries and what books are still to be acquired. It is expected that reports from the participating libraries will reach the Library of Congress by the end of the calendar year, thus enabling the various libraries concerned to work out a post-war purchasing program in the interest of American scholarship as a whole.

Preliminary moves have thus been made on two fronts. We are incorporating the Library's existing holdings of Russian materials into the general collections, under control of the public catalog. At the same time, we are preparing, in conjunction with other libraries, a program of acquisition of Russian materials which will attempt to correct existing weaknesses, not only in our own collections, but in the collections of the country as a whole.

It remains to plan for the service of these materials through a Center which will increase their usefulness, not only to specialists in the United States but to American readers generally. The project we have in mind is based upon our experience with our Hispanic Foundation—one of the most successful divisions of the Library of Congress, and one of the most effective instrumentalities of the National Government in its effort to improve cultural relations with the other Republics of this hemisphere. The Hispanic Foundation not only provides advanced reference assistance to American students of Hispanic subjects, but also encourages the interchange of scholars and of scholarly materials between the centers of American culture.

The same program would be adopted, if our efforts are successful, in the general Slavic field. We are attempting now to raise funds through private gift for the establishment of a Chair of Russian Studies and for the further establishment of Consultantships to which we may invite Russian scholars and librarians for periods of a few months or a year. In addition, we propose a limited publications program which will make the work of the Center known and useful to persons unable to visit Washington. Since this project, in its early stages, will be experimental it cannot depend upon appropriated funds. It is our hope that citizens interested in the wise development of our relations with Russia, and conscious of the importance to those relations of a sound library program, will make the initial experiment possible.

The Librarian speaks
· 1941-44

On annual reports . . .

The annual report of an agency of a
democratic government should, it seems
to me, be something more than a record and an
accounting. It should attempt to tell its readers what
the agency does and how well it does it — or at least
to provide the means of judging how well the work is
done. In the case of the Library of Congress no sum-
marizing of the work of the various administrative
subdivisions can tell what the Library does. The
functions of the Library are, broadly speaking, to
establish and maintain a collection of books and related materials adequate to the needs of its readers
and to make that collection readily available and
pertinently useful. But a collection of books is not
merely a large number of books, and the usefulness
of a collection is not measured in numbers of readers
alone or in quantity of service. A collection is a
number of books so combined among themselves
that each part supports and enriches every other
part, and so organized that every part relates to every

Excerpts from the *Statement of the Librarian of Congress in
Support of the Supplementary Appropriation for the Fiscal
Year 1941* (Washington, D.C.: Gov. Print. Off., 1942); *Report of
the Librarian of Congress for the Fiscal Year* Ended 1940
(Washington, D.C.: Gov. Print. Off., 1941); ibid., Reports for 1941,
1942, 1943, 1944 (1942–45).

other part not in terms of the part only but in terms of the whole. The usefulness of a collection is its responsiveness *as a collection* to the needs of readers, either through the finding machinery of the card trays, or through the selective lists of bibliographies, or through the learning and ingenuity of the reference librarians — its availability by rapid and intelligent service in the reading rooms, or by prompt and efficient delivery to outside users or by loan through other libraries or by the provision of photographic copies.

A book in a great library like the Library of Congress, in other words, is not merely a volume on a given subject. It is a volume on a given subject which has been selected and cataloged and fitted into a system of classification and placed upon the shelves in such a way as to make it a part of the whole body of learning as the whole body of learning is represented in that library; an atom, noble or humble, in a total structure which has a form and integrity of its own quite apart from the form and integrity of its components. It is a volume, moreover, which is present in the library not merely to be present there but as an object of use, as an instrument of learning. No library worthy of the name possesses books merely as books or for the sole purpose of possessing them. Books in the great libraries lose their physical identities, their cardboard, leatherbacked insulation from each other, and become pages in the great flow of letters and learning, so arranged and so served that, through them, learning and letters are not only preserved but brought to fullest life. There is no place in a great library for an author's vanity but only for letters and for learning brought to wholeness and to hand.

To judge, therefore, whether the work of a great library is well done from year to year it is necessary to know whether the entire collection is consistently approaching the wholeness and the harmony it can never achieve but must always labor to attain — whether the entire collection is nearer to the impossible but nevertheless imperative ideal of organic responsiveness to its reader's need. What is required for that purpose is information as to new acquisitions not in terms of their value in and of themselves but in terms of their importance to the total collection, in terms of the collection's lacks and needs and weaknesses as well as in terms of the collection's strength. What is required is an account of the library's technical procedures not in terms of an abstract technical excellence or lack of excellence but in terms of their adequacy to the integration and the responsiveness of the collection they control — an account of services to readers not in terms simply of their extensiveness as services but in terms of their relation to the collection and to the purposes for which the collection is maintained — an account of housekeeping and fiscal services which will record the statistics of expenditure and upkeep not as abstract statistics but as indications of the cost of the library's activities measured in terms of those activities.

On acquisitions . . .

Furthermore, in any great library, the collections of the library cannot be wisely and skillfully maintained without the exercise of scholarly judgment by the library staff. Books do not accumulate automatically. They must be selected. And selection, in a library which takes all human knowledge as its field and many millions of volumes as its choice, is a difficult and laborious process requiring the exercise of the greatest powers of judgment and the possession of the broadest resources of scholarship and erudition. No one man, and no haphazard group of men, can build up the collections of a library of the size of the Library of Congress. The association of many scholars in many fields is a basic necessity if the Library of Congress is to collect the books its users have a right to expect it to collect, and if the Library of Congress is to make those books humanly as well as mechanically available.

There are in these days and for this institution few amenities in book collecting. The emphasis has shifted from the reduction of *lacunae* in retrospective literature to the more serious and much more perplexing task of securing the most recent information derivable from distant parts of the world.

* * *

Additions made to the collections of a great library are a measure of its health, for they reflect the competence or incompetence, the imagination or stupor, the enthusiasm or complacency of its curators, and provide a test of its purpose. Mere *accumulation*, whether it be the accumulation of books or the accumulation of other physical objects, sets only a standard for sterility and stagnation; whereas *development*—intentional and organized and occasionally attained—is an hematogen, enriching and renewing the blood. Acquisitions, in other words, are recognizable either as sources of strength or as causes of weakness, and may be subjected to a qualitative examination.

* * *

We have not been able as yet—we may never be able—to isolate in one department all acquisitions operations, from the first interest in a book to the final shove which places it upon a shelf: from the cradle, as unkind critics might say, to the grave. We still depend, and we shall probably always depend, on subject specialists, in whatever department they may work, for purchase recommendations in the various subject fields. We have, however, succeeded in making these subject specialists functionally answerable to the Director of the Acquisitions Department for their acquisitions recommendations, even though they may be answerable to other directors for functions of a different kind. The arrangement presents difficulties to those who love to reduce organization to charts and graphs, but it has the great and counterbalancing advantage that it works.

On inventories and losses . . .

An inventory of a collection of millions of volumes is a formidable undertaking which must either withdraw from their duties a large number of employees or, if handled by a small group, must drag over so long a period as to make the findings almost meaningless. It is not particularly illuminating to know that at some time within a period of six or eight or ten years a library had books on its shelves which, added together at the end of this period, amounted to such and such a figure. The question to be answered as accurately as possible is the question of the Library's holdings at a given time. And it is this question which, in a large library, is so peculiarly difficult.

*　　*　　*

The only libraries which do not suffer considerable losses are the libraries which are able to impose rigorous and closely policed limitations on the use of their books, and the former Librarian of Congress was not a man who saw his duty in terms of restrictions and limitations. As he saw it – and I am proud to associate myself with his words – "There is a possibility that some book lent may be lost to posterity seeking it at Washington. There is a risk, to the charge of which I know but one answer: that a book used is, after all, fulfilling a higher mission than a book which is merely being preserved for possible future use."

On reference services... ..

But though it is essential that all books and other materials in a great library should be made available through catalogues, the obligations of the library do not end at that point. A catalogue is a mechanism which is wholly responsive only to those who are professionally familiar with its use. And in a great library—in a library, specifically, of close to six millions of books and pamphlets—no merely mechanical instrument can effectively serve the needs of readers, whether they are scholars who consult the collections for purposes of research or statesmen who consult them for purposes of action. In any great library, and specifically in a library as great as the Library of Congress, the library staff must be trained and prepared to mediate between the books and those who wish to consult them; to supply the statesman quickly and imaginatively with the material necessary to his purpose; to direct the scholar accurately and wisely to the editions he needs; to advise the more general reader as to the limits and the possibilities of his reading.

Number of readers and quantity of demand provide one element only. The immeasurable balance is *quality* of demand. Service to a scholar who knows his author's name and merely needs to locate his title is one thing. Service to a researcher who begins, not with an author, or with a title, or even with a subject, but with an urgent and pressing problem of government, or of raw materials, or, say, of the administration of manpower, is another.

*   *   *

The notion widely held, in the profession and out of it, that the American library catalog has largely solved the problem of library use is a notion which does not correspond to modern facts. The catalog devised by the masters of American librarianship was a magnificent machine—one of the great works of modern scholarship. But it was a machine devised to serve a reader who approached it either with an author's name or a book's title or a scholar's definition of a subject in mind; a reader moreover who, if he approached the catalog from the subject side, would have, and could take, the necessary time to run through the literature collected under his subject and determine for himself what book or books best supplied him with the things he needed.

The function of the catalog, in other words, was to put a book or a group of books in a reader's hands, the reader knowing beforehand more or less what he wanted in book terms, and having the time to secure from his books the precise material he had come to find. The difficulty now is that the reader imagined by the catalog-makers is not in every respect the reader produced by contemporary society. The modern reader, particularly in a great reference library serving the machinery of a modern state, is not infrequently a man working under great pressures of time and of responsibility, who does not know, and cannot be expected to know, what book written by what man may give him what he needs, or what subdivision of what subject may have been assigned to it by a cataloger: a man who has no time to read through a pile of several dozen volumes or even to consult the chapters neatly marked with paper markers.

Such a reader can be adequately served only by some such machinery as the lawyer now possesses to lead him to the precise authority he needs to find—or, failing that, by the human intervention of trained reference librarians working from selective bibliographies and producing, as the end product of their work, not an assembly of random references but the materials actually relevant to the solution of the problem. It is not inconceivable that narrower and more sensitive and more precise controls may in time be developed by a refinement of the classification system, or by some comparable means, but until that time the Library of Congress must provide, as well as it can, the interpreting specialists and scholars who can make the vast and rapidly increasing mass of printed matter responsive to the needs of those who require access to it for the urgent solution of complicated and intensely difficult problems of government and administration.

To measure the demand upon the Library's services to readers in these terms is to indicate what is, indeed, the fact—that the opportunities for usefulness are endless, that the Library's ability to satisfy them is limited primarily by the size of its reference staff and that the evaluation of accomplishment in statistical terms is impossible.

* * *

One of the conditions of the successful performance of a qualitative, as distinguished from a quantitative, service is some degree of selective control over the tasks to be undertaken. A reference service which undertakes to answer any inquiry from anywhere, the most childishly simple as well as the most technically complex, will shortly lose control of its operations and fail to perform its work. A selection of inquiries must be made, and the efforts of the staff must be applied where they can be most effective.

On subject bibliographies...

There are available to the users of great research libraries elaborate catalogs arranged by authors, subjects and titles, which are excellent as finding media for the stores of knowledge in their collections. These are "dictionary catalogs," compiled in a single alphabet, which possess at once the advantages and disadvantages of a dictionary discipline, for although the information contained in them is readily discoverable, and although they are comprehensive in their coverage of subject fields, the information is nevertheless (and necessarily) meager, while the coverage, in terms of actual content, is undiscriminating, uncritical, and unselective. The unfortunate result of this circumstance is that users not infrequently are overwhelmed by the very mass of material, and that they fumble through trays of cards without locating the exact references which are appropriate to their purpose. It is imperative, therefore, to supplement the resources of the catalog apparatus with annotated subject bibliographies which distinguish, cull, and appraise the merits and matter of several publications devoted to a single theme. The economies achieved by enumerative bibliography are not statistically ascertainable, but it is certain that they are increasing and that they are increasingly important.

The demand upon us for bibliographic work is often urgent and never wholly satisfied, even though all reference divisions of the Library are engaged to a greater or less extent in this labor. The bibliographies requested, moreover, cover a tremendous range of knowledge. Some inquiries are so simple and routine that a brief consultation of the public catalog suffices to prepare an adequate reply, while other needs are so large that their satisfaction requires many months of constant effort. The quality of the product also varies greatly. Some bibliographies—perhaps most of them—may be considered as performing the humble but indispensable service of midwife to research, while others constitute scholarly achievements in themselves. Most significant of all, published bibliographies make the Library's holdings known to a larger public than ever walks through the doors of the Library, and serve thousands of readers who may never come to Washington.

On processing problems ...

The services of the Library are its reasons for existence, and the quality of its collections is a measure of the facilities at hand through which the Library is equipped to serve its clientele. Underlying the collections and the services are the procedures by which materials are acquired and prepared for use. On these activities rests, in major part, the success with which the Library meets its obligations. The business operations involved in the purchasing and receiving of materials and the technical and professional procedures necessary to the preparation of material for the collections are operations with which readers are rarely familiar. They are crucial in the work of the Library, however.

*   *   *

Libraries have struggled for decades with the problem of cataloging costs. Lack of progress is primarily attributable to the difficulty of analyzing jobs so as to give meaningful measures of the work done.

New approaches to this problem which promise greater success are now being studied.

Improvements in the economy of operations depend only in part, however, on cost analysis. Reference has already been made to studies on the flow of materials through the processing operations. It is being demonstrated that these studies bring to light unnecessary steps in processing which will be eliminated. One important need for cost studies is the development of effective production standards. These are of great importance for the evaluation of the work accomplished by assistants engaged in the various operations.

The maintenance of the card catalog is a key operation in the processing activities of the Library. Many problems are involved in the arrangement and current revision of a catalog of more than ten million cards which, even under the best of conditions, can be extraordinarily confusing to the reader who attempts to make use of the catalog as a guide to the Library's collections. As difficulties experienced by readers are ascertained, efforts are made by the Library to modify its cataloging procedures. This relationship between the reader and the librarian is complex, but assurance is given that the attention of the Library is centered on the problem of discovering new keys to its resources in the interest of its readers.

* * *

In the processing of books, periodicals, manuscripts, and the great variety of other materials received by the Library, the attention of the staff devoted to this activity must be centered on three general problems. The first of the problems is the necessity for day-by-day processing of the never-ending flow of materials. The second of the problems is the still large accumulation of uncataloged arrearages. The third of the problems is the urgent necessity for reaching out after new methods of treatment which will more successfully record and interpret that share of the flood of the world's print which comes to the Library of Congress.

The third problem may well be restated—the urgent necessity for reaching out after new methods of treatment which will successfully record and interpret the flood of print which comes to the Library of Congress. This is only in part the problem of the Library of Congress. It is also a problem which we hold in common with the whole world of libraries and scholarship. This is true because the publications which come into the Library of Congress are only a small part of the total record. No one library can solve this problem alone, for it is a problem crucial to the welfare of democratic society. The Library of Congress is prepared to devote an increasing share of its energies to a cooperative attack upon this problem.

*   *   *

As the president of a great American university has put it, American libraries as a whole are either doing far too much or far too little in their efforts to catalog the vast modern flow of printed and near-printed materials. Libraries should either have the courage of their convictions and demand in season and out that they be provided with the armies of catalogers who would be required to apply the existing procedures to the swelling flood of print, or they should admit that the procedures are outmoded and devote all their efforts to the search for a solution adapted to the realities of the work to be done and the time and manpower available to do it.

The prescription is a harsh one, but it may be the part of wisdom to swallow it. At the very least, the sickness should be admitted and the symptoms studied. It is at least possible that if the profession would candidly face the fact that present cataloging methods are nineteenth century methods devised for forms of print which no longer constitute the bulk of library accessions, and for categories of readers who constitute a part only of present and potential library clienteles, a solution satisfactory to the profession could be found. What is needed is a form of control adapted to the mass and form of materials libraries now take in and useful to the readers who consult those materials—a form superior both qualitatively and quantitatively to forms now in use—a form precise enough to serve the specialist but not so cabalistic or elaborate as to confuse the general reader.

Such a form, or such a combination of forms, may be difficult in the extreme to find, but the problem is a problem librarians are trained to attack. The first step would seem to be a review of existing procedures. This the Library of Congress has now attempted.

At some appropriate future time—certainly not until well after the war—a related question should also be raised with the principal American libraries and learned bodies. The Library of Congress system of classification plays a part in American scholarship of which not all American scholars are aware. It should be reexamined in the light of the scholarly and scientific work of the past several generations and brought more nearly into line with present conceptions. Ideally a basic organization of knowledge of this nature should be the work of a national academy of arts and sciences representative of the entire learned community. Lacking a single body of this extensive character staffed to undertake so difficult a labor, a congress of the various disciplines might well be called to direct its execution. The present practice by which "subject headings" are "assigned" by the staff of the Library's Subject Cataloging Division leaves something to be desired both in the Library and out of it. No matter how learned the Library's specialists may be—and some of them are men of an extraordinary breadth of learning—they cannot be familiar with the development of ideas and conceptions in all the disciplines nor can they project the past history of ideas into the future as the masters of a subject field can do. That the problem has something more than academic interest at this time is indicated by the fact that the Library's Subject Cataloging Division has been obliged in the past year to adopt five times as many new headings as it adopted in the average year of the past decade.

On circulation statistics . . .

It is difficult, if not impossible, to give meaning to statistics of circulation. They can, it is true, represent the *volume* of business during a given year, and that volume can be compared with the business of other years. They indicate also the frequency with which stack attendants removed books from the shelves, the count of persons who crossed the thresholds of the reading rooms, the number of loans made to borrowers; and yet the fact remains that there is nothing so completely anonymous as a number.

Statistics of circulation do not explain the uses made of books, or why one book was preferred to another; neither do they afford a clue to the nature of the readers or to the importance of their work.

On administrative organization . . .

Administrative organization is not, or should not be, an end in itself. Nevertheless some account of it has its inevitable place in any attempt to describe a living institution. Without an understanding of anatomy it is difficult to picture function. And what is true in biology is true in government as well.

*   *   *

A good deal – perhaps too much – has been said in earlier reports about the reorganization of the Library which began in 1940. Although the reorganization is not yet completed, it is possible this year to describe its results in terms of the over-all pattern which has now emerged. The object in view throughout was the effective control of the Library's numerous and various activities through administrative subdivisions created for logical and functional purposes and enjoying a high degree of functional autonomy but responsible nevertheless, and effectively responsible, to the Librarian. Stated in other words, the object was to preserve the unity and singleness of the Library as a whole, while, at the same time, allowing the various and diverse activities of the Library to develop freely in their several ways under the direction of the numerous specialists and experts.

The problem was not unlike the problem recently faced by some, at least, of the great American universities. An earlier academic tendency toward specialization and departmentalization has, in certain cases, overreached itself and several universities have thought it necessary to restore, by various devices, the free commerce between the different fields of knowledge which excessive departmentalization, like excessive nationalism, destroys. It was and is the great good fortune of the Library of Congress that the bulk of its materials are still held in the general collections despite the tendency, ten and fifteen years ago, to set up special divisions with special collections of their own. The basis for sound reorganization therefore existed. The difficulty was the difficulty of providing new administrative forms which would make so vast a unit responsive to a central direction.

*   *   *

It is unnecessary to remark that the broad administrative organization accomplished by these methods depends for its success, like all administrative devices, on the human beings involved. "Administrative machinery" is not machinery but people, and "administrative channels" are not channels but human relationships. An efficient and effective agency is an agency in which administrative forms are recognized for what they are—forms and not substance. The moment "channels" dominate communications or administrative charts tyrannize over administrative action, the official joints congeal and the institution hardens. It is generally understood and agreed within the Library, I think, that the logic of the Library's new organization is not a deadening logic of this nature. Any member of the Library staff who wants to see the Librarian can see him regardless of blue prints, and any piece of Library business which cannot accommodate itself to channels will get itself done regardless of channels. The organization as now established should make most of our work easier to perform. In the unusual instance when it doesn't, the work will come first and the organization after.

On library salaries . . .

The Library of Congress lost hundreds of men and women, as it should have lost them, to the armed services and to the war agencies. But it lost other hundreds of men and women whom it should not have lost, for it lost them, not because of the war, but because the Library, as I have previously noted in these Reports, is at a permanent disadvantage in competing with other employers: it is unable to offer equal salaries for equal work.

The explanation of the Library's relatively lower salaries is to be found in two facts, the one historical, the other psychological.

The historical reason is that the Library has not been reclassified as a whole for eighteen years. With the helpful cooperation of the Civil Service Commission a resurvey was begun in 1941 which the Commission expects to complete, despite the present heavy demands upon its staff, by the end of the calendar year.

*   *   *

The psychological reason for low Library salaries is to be found in the *qualitative* evaluation of library work *as such* — a reason which affects library salaries not only in the Government but throughout the country. Professional work in the law, or professional work in finance, or professional work in economics is assumed to exceed in value professional work in the assembling, organization, interpretation, and service of the printed materials without which the work of the specialists in law or finance or economics would be impossible. The result is that legal positions or financial positions or economic positions in the Government are classified incomparably higher than the positions of those whose professional skill secures and makes serviceable the essential materials through which the lawyers and the economists work.

*   *   *

There is, I submit, no substantial reason for this discrepancy if civil-service salaries for professional work are to be determined upon the basis of the difficulty and responsibility of the work done. It is true that lawyers in private practice sometimes receive very large incomes and that economic and financial advisers in private business are paid high salaries, but it is not true that work in these fields is inherently more difficult than work done by professional librarians or that the responsibilities are greater. Neither is it true that good men are more difficult to find and must consequently be offered higher salaries. Precisely because its salaries are what they are, the librarian's profession has attracted relatively few men and women possessing the qualifications that the profession's service, particularly in government, now so badly needs.

*   *   *

The Library has lost many man-years of time through its inability to fill positions which stood vacant for days and weeks because no one with the academic and professional qualifications required could afford to accept the salaries offered.

*   *   *

Moreover, the Library's loss is not a loss in terms of time alone. The Library has suffered an additional and more serious loss to its resources of accumulated experience. The working capital of a highly technical agency like the Library of Congress is the accumulated experience of its staff. When workers are lost, experience is lost with them. When replacements are hired, experience is drained off again, for experienced members of the staff must attempt to communicate their experience to the new arrivals at the expense of time devoted to their own work.

*   *   *

It is a wastage which can be largely stopped by a corrective as simple as it is equitable—the equalization of salary levels as between government work in books and letters and government work in such comparable professional fields as economics and finance and law.

The library
and the nation
· 1945

The purpose of this volume, as I understand it, is to examine books and their writing and their reading and the institutions which serve them — particularly the institutions which serve them — under the aspect, not of eternity, but of war. It is a valid and interesting, even an exciting, purpose. Any continuing institution can be usefully studied as it appears in times of stress and danger — the flashlight moments when the shadows and surfaces are caught in vivid and unconscious tension.

But it is implicit in the statement of the purpose of this book that what we are examining is the *appearance* of the institution as it presents itself in the blue-white glare of danger and reacting effort. Such continuing institutions as libraries do not change the substantial character of their services or of their operations in time of war. What changes is the appearance of their functions to those who see those functions in the new light — the sharp perspective.

Which means, of course, to those who are aware of the new light and who see by its perspective. If one is considering, for example, how libraries appear under the aspect of the present war to the citizens of the United States, it would be the part of wisdom to take account at the outset of the fact that there are considerable aggregations of American citizens who have been kept as far from that light — as far from

First published in Pierce Butler, ed., *Books and Libraries in Wartime* (Chicago: Univ. of Chicago Press, 1945), p.141–54. Copyright 1945 by the University of Chicago. All rights reserved.

an understanding of the great fighting issues and the deep fighting realities of the war—as a group of notorious newspapers, published for propaganda rather than news by prejudiced owners rather than by unprejudiced journalists, can keep them. And by the same sign, if one is considering how libraries look to librarians under the aspect of the present war, one would be wise to distinguish at the outset between those librarians, on the one hand (and they are numerous, and not least in this city), who have understood from the start that this war is a war in which the things of the mind are inextricably and inevitably involved, and those, on the other hand, who believe that war, even Fascist war, is in some enchanted manner none of their business—that the only duty of a librarian is to thicken the indifferent walls of his library until it becomes a kind of bomb-proof shelter for intellectual irresponsibility in which no echo of the agony of mankind—indeed, no echo of mankind—can ever penetrate.

But though it is the part of wisdom to remember that not all librarians and not all users of libraries are personally and immediately aware of the war, it is nevertheless possible and useful to examine the changed appearance of the library in the public eye in time of war and possible also to consider its changed aspect in the eye of the librarian.

The public, needless to say, is never particularly conscious of its libraries, peace or war. Men who call themselves civilized are, generally speaking, *for* libraries as they are *for* virtue. No one, that is to say, dreams of attacking libraries as such. Put to the question, no one but a professional Watch-and-Warder or a professional purifier of his neighbor's morals, a dogmatist or a prude afraid of print and words or a reactionary politician afraid of the people's knowledge—afraid, that is to say, of the people—would speak against a library. But at the same time no one, even in a self-consciously civilized society, does very much about libraries. As witness the fact that library salaries are among the meanest paid by American communities to those who serve them. Editorial friends of American libraries—and they are, thank God, numerous and articulate—praise the library as the poor man's university, and the country applauds. But deep in their hearts the readers of such eloquent editorials are convinced that the metaphor is only a metaphor—that you do not need a library of hundreds of thousands, not to say millions, of books to enable the poor young man to read his way to wisdom.

Fundamentally, the popular view of the libraries, and particularly the greatest libraries, is the view that they are cultural luxuries, good because they relate to learning, but luxuries notwithstanding. It is not for nothing that the greatest library in the British Commonwealth is called the British Museum. In the popular view the books in the British Museum—or in the Library of Congress or in the Bibliothèque Nationale—the vast collections of reference materials of all sorts and kinds—are museum objects—rare and therefore no doubt valuable, but of an obscure and debatable usefulness.

What war—modern war at least—does to the popular view of great libraries is to drive home the fact to those who are willing to see it that whatever a great reference library may be to any given individual, or any group of individuals, it is a vital necessity to a *nation*. War, modern war at least, cannot be fought without the most complete library resources. No library resources can ever be too complete for the necessities of a great industrial state engaged in a war which involves all its facilities, all its manpower, and all its knowledge. We know now, whatever we may have thought we knew before, that no island in any ocean of the earth is too remote or too small or too inconspicuous to be of vital concern to the planning and operating staffs in a war fought with modern airpower and modern seapower, to say nothing of modern power on the land. The Library of Congress knows to its cost what its failure to collect over the last century and a half every scrap of printed and manuscript material on the islands of the Pacific has meant to its service to the government of the United States.

What is true of geography and climate and meteorological data is also true of technological and commercial and industrial and economic publications. There is no material, for example, bearing upon industrial practices, plant locations, systems of transportation, resources of raw material, resources of manpower, and the like, in any part of the Axis-occupied world, which is not potentially or actually a source of military intelligence of the first importance.

It is a matter of public interest, but of limited public knowledge, that one of the first specific wartime steps taken by our government in the field of military intelligence in this war, was the establishment in the Library of Congress, in co-operation with the Co-ordinator of Information, as he was then called — now the Director of the Office of Strategic Services — of a Division of Special Information, which brought to Washington to work in and with the collections of the Library of Congress, and in and with materials specifically collected for the purpose, a group of the foremost historians, economists, and geographers in the United States. When the full story of the Office of Strategic Services can be told, it will appear that the Office's Division of Research and Analysis, first under President Baxter of Williams and then under Professor William Langer of Harvard, performed a labor of integration and orientation of knowledge of the very first importance to the conduct of the war. In that work the collections of the Library of Congress were the principal reliance. But the collections of the Library of Congress, had they been more complete and more universal than they were, would have been of greater service to the Office of Strategic Services and thus to the armed services. One definite lesson of the war so far as the collections of the Library of Congress are concerned, is not that eighteen million books and pieces are a great many books and pieces, but that eighteen million books and pieces – at least those particular eighteen million – are not large enough or complete enough in their coverage for the country they are supposed to serve.

The first thing the war has driven home, then, to the members of the general public who have thought about these things, and who are at all aware of the services of libraries in the war, is the fact that the great libraries exist not only for individual readers, or for university faculties, or student bodies, but for the nation; and that the nation cannot live without them. It is not, I grant you, a new conception.

Those in my profession who follow the annual reports of librarians and who read the learned journals have been aware for a long time that in a society as complex as ours the great reference libraries are an essential part of the functioning mechanism of the nation's life. Not only are they essential to scholarship, but they are essential to operations which are not ordinarily considered to be related to scholarship. All the war has done, therefore, is to demonstrate a fact previously known. But the proof, because it has been dramatic and because there is no answer to it, is proof that we may hope will not be forgotten.

You cannot destroy seventeen million books in western Russia, you cannot liquidate in effect the library facilities of Poland, you cannot destroy twenty-five libraries in China, without making people whose imaginations react a little to what they read in the newspapers aware of the fact that it is a disaster to lose your library facilities.

It is easy enough to take the great libraries for granted when they present themselves to the public eye as solid stone buildings, with solid metal doors, solidly constructed on squares and corners in solid cities which have had them so long that they have forgotten there was ever a time when they did not have them. It is another thing altogether to look at the New York Public Library or the Boston Public Library or the great library of this University or the Library of Congress or the British Museum with the libraries of Poland and China and parts of Italy in mind.

Anyone who has seen the British Museum since the blitz can no longer think of libraries at home with the easy feeling of self-confidence and assurance for the future with which we usually regard them. And anyone who has considered what the life of this country would be had it suffered in its libraries any part of the loss and destruction which has been suffered by, let us say, the nation of Poland, will understand what its libraries mean to a nation. If the Library of Congress were destroyed, it would be necessary to attempt, by every means and at any cost, the impossible labor of its reconstruction, for the government of the United States, quite literally and quite simply, could not conduct its business without the Library's collections.

But there is an additional and perhaps an even more dramatic demonstration of the importance of the great libraries to the nations they serve. That demonstration is offered by the Nazi party in Germany. It is now a truism, though a truism which some of us seem to be rather eager to forget, that the war made by the Nazis is not an imperialistic war in the ordinary sense. It is not, that is to say, a war for the conquest of territory—a war for the direct conquest of territory. The spoils of war for which the Nazis fight are men's minds. They believe that the historic culture of the world—of the Western world at least—is corrupt and rotten and can be replaced by an anti-culture of their making. They believe, and with excellent reason, that if they can impose their Fascist anti-culture upon the minds and habits of a great majority of living men, the territories and the raw materials and the seaports and all the rest will follow of themselves. But they also realize—and this is the unconscious tribute they pay the libraries of the world—that to impose an anti-culture upon Europe and the West, it is necessary first to destroy the great repositories of the historical culture of those countries and the men and women who serve them.

The murders of the teachers, the writers, the intellectuals; the burning of books and the pillage and destruction of libraries in Poland, the one country in which the Nazis thought their plan could be played out, are open and visible proof to anyone who cares to look at it that, in the opinion at least of those who hate the forms of society to which we are attached, the principal weapons and the principal defenses of a free nation are the books, and the organizations of books, which serve it.

What the general public may have learned from the war, then, is the lesson that the great libraries are essential to the security of free nations. If that lesson is learned, it will mean a great deal to the future of the librarian's profession and to the future of the culture which depends upon free institutions for its life and its vitality.

What the librarians may have learned is something larger—that the security of libraries, and through them the security of learning, and through the security of learning, the peace of the world, may well depend upon the service of libraries not to their own nations only but to the world at large. Which is another way of saying that the lesson librarians may have learned from this war—those librarians who look at libraries in the true light of this war—may very well be this: that the world cannot survive in freedom and safety and enlightenment unless librarians alter basically their conception of their responsibility for the materials in their charge.

That, I am well aware, is a large saying which requires demonstration; and a saying I should like to try to demonstrate if I can because it is the most emphatic conclusion I bring back from a month in England and from many days and nights of talk with people in that country who have this, among other related problems, very heavily upon their minds.

My demonstration would run something like this: If you assume—what is to be assumed because it is a fact—that library facilities in large parts of eastern Europe and western Russia have been almost altogether destroyed; if you assume, what is a fact, that the libraries of the Far East have been very largely destroyed and their materials with them; and if you assume, what wisdom and prudence would require you to assume, that in the process of the invasion and in the process of Nazi retreat there will be an even greater and even broader destruction of library materials throughout Axis-occupied areas— throughout Europe as a whole—then I think you come inevitably to the conclusion that a situation now exists, or will exist at the end of the war, which will require a restatement of the responsibilities of those who direct the surviving libraries of the world. There will exist, at the end of the war, in large parts of the world, areas in which library facilities which are essential to the operation of a complicated modern society are no longer available. There will exist, in other words, in large areas of the world, precisely the situation the Fascists intended to create—a situation in which they hope to be able to breed out of darkness and ignorance the kind of anti-culture which can only thrive on darkness and ignorance. (None of us, I suppose, is foolish enough to think that the defeat of Fascist arms will end the threat of fascism everywhere in the world.)

Now if it is true that you face a situation at the end of the war in which large areas of the world are without access to facilities they must have to function as parts of contemporary civilization, and if it is true that that situation is a situation which the free countries of the world cannot tolerate, you then come to the necessary conclusion that something must be done about it—that those areas of the world must again be given freedom of access to the materials they require.

And something has of course been done. Plans have been made. Funds have been received from foundations. Duplicates have been collected from surviving libraries. Appeals for books have been issued. But none of these things touches the heart of the real problem. All libraries in the Axis-dominated world and in Axis-occupied territories will of course need materials from 1938 and 1939 on, and the plans already made will be most helpful to them. I am not talking, however, about that situation. I am talking about the situation which will exist where libraries have been altogether destroyed—where the basic reference materials which make a library no longer exist. There, I submit, the methods thus far suggested fall far short of meeting the need, and new and different forms of aid must be found.

But what forms? Money alone will not suffice. The materials which will be needed to restore ruined libraries are not for sale. No publisher publishes them. No bookseller has them in stock. They exist only in other libraries, and it is only through the co-operation and collaboration of other libraries that they can be made available.

Only if the principal librarians of the world could agree upon the proposition that they hold their materials as trustees, not for the faculties of their universities, not for the student bodies of their colleges, not for the citizens of their towns, not even for the citizens of their nations, but for the entire generation of living men, and only if their acceptance of that proposition could be implemented by the known, tried, and tested methods of interlibrary loan over international boundaries, would it be possible in my opinion to solve the problem.

Now many, perhaps most, librarians are men and women who have thought a good deal about library problems and who are familiar with the difficulties in the way of any such proposal. Am I proposing to ask librarians in various parts of the world to loan materials abroad which they are ordinarily unwilling to allow out of their treasure-rooms? Do I contemplate a universal, world-wide Union Catalogue in five, six, or twenty different alphabets in order to enable people who want books to find out where they are?

You will probably have very many objections and questions, but those two, since they are obvious and clear, I would like to deal with. So far as the first is concerned, the answer of course is "No." You would expect to apply to an international program of interlibrary loan exactly the same kind of principles you would apply in intranational interlibrary loans. As you know, international interlibrary loan is not new under the sun. It is an operation that has been practiced in moderation for some time. One does not expect libraries to send out of their treasure-rooms to distant parts books that they ordinarily do not allow to leave the room itself. On the contrary, you would expect loaning libraries to use photographic copies in such cases. The rapid international transportation which will exist after the war will have an extraordinary effect on this kind of intercourse between nations. It may well be possible to send photographic materials and even books to India and to other remote parts of the world in a matter of days if not of hours; but certainly a matter of days.

The problem of discovering where, in what country, in whose hands a given book is to be found is a rather more difficult problem, but, again, a problem which can be solved. A world Union Catalogue is probably impossible at the present time. The national Union Catalog in the Library of Congress now includes, after many years of labor and the expenditure of large sums of money, no more than ten to twelve million titles out of an estimated eighteen million. A world Union Catalogue in the various alphabets of the world presents far greater difficulties.

But one thing can be done. Regional union catalogues with regional divisions of responsibility can be established. If the nations of the various regions of the world would agree to possess in their regional libraries the printed materials necessary to an understanding of the history, the intellectual life, the background, the present activities of the region, regional union catalogues could be organized which, taken together, would give the necessary central control.

A by-product of any such arrangement would be an improvement in acquisition practices, and an economy in acquisition funds, in all large reference libraries everywhere. If there existed in India a central library or a group of libraries which agreed to maintain the pamphlet material, the ephemeral material, the printed material necessary to an understanding of India, the Library of Congress, for example, would be freed of the responsibility of securing material of this kind for its own collection. I do not mean by this that the Library of Congress would become a nationalistic library interested only in American material. Quite the contrary, the Library of Congress would be able to use its necessarily limited acquisitions resources to acquire the materials needed from abroad for its long-range purposes, rather than spending large amounts of money to obtain materials needed for an answer to an urgent call which could have been satisfied quite as well by loan had loan been possible.

Now it seems to me conceivable that some such system of responsibility, if proposed by an international conference properly accredited to consider the matter, might be accepted. It seems to me also that if you had such a basis of regional responsibility, you would need no great central international organization to run a system of international interlibrary loans. And it seems to me, finally, that if you could secure these two preliminary elements or procedures, it might be possible to set up a system of world circulation of library materials which would be of the most tremendous importance, not only to libraries and librarians, but to the understanding of each other of peoples who must understand each other if they are going to live together in peace.

Basically, if I may come back to my original proposition, you would have agreement upon a proposal which, it seems to me, is a proposal the world has now grown up to and must face and adopt. The time is long, long past in my view and in the view of most of my colleagues when librarians can afford to act as competitors in the business of trying to secure materials for their particular self-glory and gratification. We are all human and we all like to secure materials which cannot be found elsewhere. We all like to say that our collections in this, that, and the other field are among the greatest, or are indeed the greatest in the world. But nevertheless we have long since passed the time when it was possible for a librarian to play with a library as though it were a rich man's toy. Libraries are now so fundamentally and essentially integrated with the actual going life of the society to which we belong that that kind of self-indulgence cannot be tolerated. Librarians must treat their materials as though they belonged to the entire generation of living men, not because it is more generous to treat them that way, but because it is impossible to treat them in any other way. In the world's libraries, whatever may be true of the world's economic system or its money system or its politics, there are no frontiers.

Libraries
and mass communication
· 1950

Looking at this beautiful and exciting building I realize again what happens in the communities of this Republic as the devoted men and women — women for the most part — who care about libraries and know why they care about them undertake the tasks they have set themselves. I know a little of what was accomplished by the lovely lady who acts as chairman of this meeting — a new friend of mine but an old friend of yours. I know what your children did: and what a heart-lifting thing that is! To say they collected a million pennies is astonishing enough: what is more astonishing is the fact that they wanted to collect them, and for this purpose — for a library of their own.

I suppose one would have to say that this building — the building the pennies built, with the help of quite a number of generously given dollars — is a symbol of something larger than itself — a symbol of what we are and can do when we set our minds to it. But it is also something more than symbol, because it is not only a building. It is also a library. And a library, at this particular moment in the history of our kind, is one of the most important things on earth.

You might define a library, adequately enough, as

*An excerpt from informal remarks made by Archibald MacLeish at the dedication of the Fitchburg (Massachusetts) Youth Library on 28 September 1950. Mr. MacLeish was introduced by Mrs. George Wallace.

a place you go to to read books. It is also, of course, a place you go to to read picture magazines and to look up information of one kind or another, but more and more, as you get older and look back, you will find yourself thinking of a given library as the place in which you read such and such a book: *Moby Dick*, perhaps (I can remember the precise place on Brattle Street in Cambridge where I first heard of *Moby Dick* and the shelf in Widener Library where I found it), or Emerson's *Journals* or, maybe, for later generations, Eliot's *Four Quartets* or those beautiful first short stories of Hemingway's or your first page of Faulkner.

As we move into an age of mass communication, we move also into an age of mass-produced minds—look-alike mentalities. People are processed by television programs carpentered for the lowest common denominator, and television's estimate of the lowest common denominator is low indeed. We begin to resemble each other, not only in our clothes, but in our ideas and at a level of intelligence at which no one needs to be excluded, not even a retarded child. The result is not only that mass vulgarity increases, but that the sameness of mass vulgarity stifles everything. The "appetite for singularity"—to use Pierre Emanuel's marvelous phrase—begins to leave us and with it the originality, the differences between one man and another, which make life exciting, vivid, alive.

It is here that the reading of books—the library as the place in which books are read—becomes important as it has never been before. It is in books and by means of books that an escape from the sameness and suffocation of television and the other mass media is possible. In a book you touch, not a generalized, universalized opinion which is standard orthodoxy for the moment, but a man at the most living moment of his life—the moment when he is struggling with those aspects of his human experience which have moved him most, puzzled him most — those aspects which define him as a man, as a self different from other selves.

It is for that reason, or so it seems to me, that libraries have now become, not simply useful institutions, desirable services to have in a community, evidences of local culture, but something far more important — the one means by which a vivid, different, living life may still be available to all men — the means to human intelligence, human imagination, human passion, not at its lowest and dullest and most commonplace, but at its highest, its most human.

A tower
which will not yield
· 1956

There may be, indeed there are certain to be, men and women in this audience who will consider the ceremony performed
here today nothing but ceremony: the kind of academic occasion which academic people are always
thinking up to justify the dragooning of yet another
audience to sit uncomfortably through yet another
hour to listen respectfully (more or less) to yet another academic speaker making yet another academic speech. Why dedicate a library—even a library as impressive as this—even a library built to
serve the needs of a college as notable in its past as
Carleton and as hopeful in its future? Libraries are
undoubtedly respectable institutions and necessary
parts of colleges and universities. Their construction
should be an occasion for congratulation all around.
But why make more of it than that? Why *dedicate* a
building full of books?

But the students of this college, having heard their
distinguished president on the subject, will have little difficulty with the answer to that question. One
dedicates a new library in the United States today
because the building of a new library in the United
States today is itself an act of dedication. It commits

Address delivered at the dedication of the Carleton College Library, Northfield, Minn., 22 September 1956. First published in
the *ALA Bulletin* 50:649–54 (November 1956). Reprinted courtesy Carleton College.

a man or an institution or a community to one side rather than the other side of the profound spiritual struggle in which our generation is engaged – the spiritual civil war, if I may call it that, which quietly but bitterly divides the country.

The reason will be obvious to anyone who considers what a library actually is – or, rather, what the word has come to mean on our continent over the past half century or so. We can no longer use it to designate those towering rooms, lined from floor to ceiling with yellow leather, which our houses used to contain because our houses no longer contain them, and no one would think of using it to describe the four foot shelf behind the television screen where six best sellers, still in their dust jackets, lean against a pair of roller skates. A library to us is something more and something different. It is many books, but it is also many *kinds* of books: as many books of as many kinds as can be gathered. Where the private library of the eighteenth and nineteenth centuries was a *selection*, the library as we think of it, the academic or public library of the twentieth century, is a *collection*. Where once the criterion of choice was one man's preference of the books which interested him or with which he felt comfortable, today the criterion of choice is a disinterested completeness within the limits of a practicable relevance. Where once a library admitted only those books of which its owner approved, excluding all those whose language offended him or whose doctrines contradicted his own, today a library – what we call a library – includes every book which falls within the limits of the library's concern, and the library's means, whether it pleases the librarian or not and whether or not its conclusions agree with his.

A library's subject field may be limited: some of the finest libraries in the United States today are what librarians call special libraries. But to no aggregation of books, no matter what its scope, do we wholeheartedly accord that proud title, which determines its content by other criteria than those of substance and relevance. The honor of the modern American librarian is the completeness as well as the worth of his collection. He would no more suppress a relevant and substantial book because it was offensive to himself personally or to his employer or to those who attempt to influence his employer than a college scientist would suppress a part of the evidence of his laboratory because it disappointed his preconceptions or disturbed the board of overseers or outraged the convictions of the loudest alumni. A modern American librarian regards himself as a trustee of the printed record of his civilization, or of so much of it as his means and his mission permit him to collect, and he would regard any exclusion from his collection of a relevant book or class of books as a falsification of the record and a breach of trust.

The consequence is that any American library — any institution we would call a library — any institution called a library whose opening decent men would solemnize — will inevitably contain books with whose arguments and conclusions many Americans, even, conceivably, all Americans, will violently disagree, as well as books whose language and whose observations of human conduct millions of us will find offensive. There will be books on political theory, all kinds of political theory including the political theory of Karl Marx. There will be books on religion, all kinds of religion including the religion of cannibals and of Protestants like myself. There will be books on art, all kinds of art including the art which produces apoplexy among Senators. There will be books in which the observation of life includes the observation of love, and books in which the observation of love keeps the eyelid open long after most of us would modestly have let it fall. There will be all sorts and kinds of books having nothing whatever in common with each other but the fact that it is these books — these and the others that could be added to them if means permitted — which contain among themselves the vast and various record of human perception, human speculation, human questioning, human doubt, human wonder, human creativeness which constitutes the memory and the fact of our human civilization.

To open a library, a modern American library, to its public of students or citizens is therefore to open a kind of Pandora's box, a box of variety. Hope is here, beauty is here, wisdom is here, but there are other stinging buzzing things beside. There are doubts which may not have been felt before. There are questions which may never before have been asked. There are old errors long since recognized as such and new errors which might conceivably be truths. There are windows into corridors of the soul which have not yet been entered and glimpses into miraculous labyrinths of the body which have not been guessed at. There are shadows and shinings of emotions never sensed or seen. And all these whirling, humming things, moreover, even the best of them, even beauty, even wisdom, may be dangerous. Men have been driven mad by too much truth. Men have been debauched by beauty. And as for the power of error, no one doubts that it exists and that mankind is wonderfully vulnerable to it. Have we not the spectacle in our own day of half the world persuaded by error to accept the slavery of the self?

So that the opening of a library is, in the most literal sense of the term, an invitation to danger. But it is also something more than that, and it is the something more I wish to speak of. Carleton College does not merely invite its students to risk themselves in this new building. It assures them at the same time — and it assures the world as well — that it believes the risks thus taken is the road to life. It affirms by this stone and steel and glass that it is a good and desirable thing for men and women, young as well as old, to have access to books of all kinds and of all opinions and to come to their own conclusions; that it is a good and desirable thing for men and women, young as well as old to examine heretical arguments as well as orthodox arguments and to decide for themselves which is right and which is wrong; that it is a good and desirable thing for men and women, young as well as old, to learn how life has looked to all kinds and conditions of observers of life, the despairing as well as the hopeful, the sensuous as well as the ascetic, and to determine for themselves which aspect of life is truth and which aspect of life is misconception: which is abhorrent and which is beautiful.

And it is precisely in this affirmation that the dedication we are seeking here consists. For to affirm what the structure of this library affirms is to commit oneself to one of the deepest and most courageous of all human beliefs. It is to commit oneself to a belief in the intelligence and the power to discriminate of the human mind. If you assert that all the opinions, all the perceptions, all the visions, all the arguments, all the images, are to be made available, insofar as you can gather them, to any mind which wishes to search them out, you are asserting at the same time that you believe the mind which searches them out is capable of judging among them and arriving at sensible conclusions. You are putting your trust, that is to say, not in indoctrination and dogma — not in the conclusions of other and earlier men which have now achieved the authority of accepted doctrine — but in the mind itself which is the instrument of all conclusions, and in the act of mind, which is also an act of spirit, by which the image of the world, generation after generation, is recreated.

Stated in the usual commonplaces of philosophic discourse such a dedication may seem neither particularly daring nor particularly new. Belief in the freedom of the mind—for this, I suppose, is what the philosophers would call it—is something of a platitude in Western dialectic. Theoretically we all of us believe in the freedom of the mind, if for no other reason than that the Communists don't believe in it. Theoretically, also, we are all of us aware that our Republic was founded upon a belief in the freedom of the mind and that the fundamental law which holds our Republic together guarantees that freedom. All this, however, is theory only. There is also fact. And fact tells a very different story. The fact is that the official philosophic agreement of all Americans on the principle of freedom of the mind covers a profound and bitter disagreement which, since the Second War, has divided us far more deeply than most of us are willing to admit. There are few Americans as yet who are willing openly to attack the Constitution and the tradition of individual liberty which it incorporates. But there have been increasing numbers of our fellow citizens who have questioned in recent years the specific Constitutional guarantees of individual freedom established in the Bill of Rights. And a surprising proportion of our people are today engaged in activities, such as the attempted suppression of books and opinions by boycott and by economic pressures of various kinds, which openly violate the spirit if not the letter of the Constitutions of the Federal Government and the several States.

In this situation the affirmation of belief in the freedom of the inquiring mind which the opening of a new library implies is anything but an affirmation of the obvious. On the contrary it is an affirmation which some Americans would regard, if they spelled its implications out, as an impudent affront. Here is a city, here is a college, which says to its citizens or its students: you may read what you please even if what you choose to read is *Das Kapital* or Ernest Hemingway or D. H. Lawrence or the *Ulysses* of Joyce. You may know whatever you choose to know; even the facts of Soviet life; even the reveries of Molly Bloom. You may read and you may know because you have a right as a free man to read and know—because your intelligence depends on your reading and knowing—because the safety of the Republic depends on your intelligence. This, to the boycotter and suppresser, is dangerous and subversive talk. He does not believe in intelligence; what he believes in is the Truth and the Truth he knows already. As for the Republic, if the Republic needs to be saved the Marines will save it or the FBI or a Congressional Committee. There is no need for the citizens, young or old, to read opinions other than the accepted opinions, or to imagine life in terms other than the accepted terms, and the institution which invites them to do either is unAmerican.

One wonders, incidentally, what these people think, if they ever do think, of the seal and symbol of the country for which they claim to speak. The eagle is a bird chiefly notable for the catholicity of its vision. It hangs at a great height in clear air where a whole valley, a whole mountain, is spread out beneath it, and nothing stirs in all that country-side which it does not see. Its passion is to see. Its life is to see. That other, clumsy, grounded bird which deals with every new experience of the world by covering its eyes with sand and exposing its nude enormous anatomy to the weapons and the wind was never considered worthy of a place on the great seal of the United States until our time. Today it has become the symbol of the selectors of text books in a number of American states and the emblem of most veterans' committees. But the eagle is still aloft there in the federal air. Will it stay, one wonders, when it sees these other clumsy frightened creatures burrowing with their beaks and chins to hide the actualities of the earth?

But this, as I say, is an incidental matter. What concerns us here—and we may thank God for it—is not the folly of the frightened but the meaning of the act of faith. The frightened are important to us only because they make the act of faith come clear. And how clear they make it come! One has only to consider what is really in issue between the offerers of books and the withholders of the books to see what the offering of books, the making available of books, means to this Republic and to the free civilization in which this Republic exists. To withhold books, to suppress books, to censor books, to deny the people of a town or of a state or of the country the right to read books as they choose to read them, is to question the basic assumption of all self-government which is the assumption that the people are capable of governing themselves: that the people, that is to say, are capable of examining the evidence for themselves and making up their own minds and coming to their own conclusions. The unstated pretension of all those who undertake to withhold books is the pretension that someone else knows better than the people: that the Chicago Archdiocesan Council of Catholic Women with its monthly blacklist of books knows better than the people; that the police chiefs of various towns and cities with their extra-legal threats to booksellers and libraries know better than the people; that the Attorney General of Massachusetts, should a bill pass directing him to establish a code "regulating and defining the permissive content of books, pamphlets etc." would know better than the people. It is the nerve-center, the heart, of democracy which is struck at by these practices and measures, for the heart of democracy is the right of a people to make up their minds for themselves. And, by the same sign, it is democracy itself, at its heart, at its center, which is strengthened whenever a free choice of books is made available to the people—whenever the people are told in their towns, in their colleges: Here are the books! Read them as you please! Make up your own minds! Determine your own destiny! Be free!

It is for this reason that the opening of a new library is no longer the merely architectural event which it would have been in the days when Andrew Carnegie was dotting the American landscapes with those placid domes of his. What were once peaceful establishments secluding themselves behind their marble animals and their metal mottoes and the enormous names of those happy authors whom they chose for more or less eternal remembrance, have become strong points and pill boxes along the extended and dangerous frontier where the future of free institutions is being fought out, day after day, in minor skirmishes rarely noticed in the public press and tactfully deprecated, when they are recorded at all, in the various professional publications. It would be difficult, I think, to overestimate the debt owed by the party of freedom in the United States today to the unknown and unsung librarians who, with little backing from their fellow citizens, and with less economic security than would encourage most of the rest of us to be brave, have held an exposed and vulnerable front through ten of the most dangerous years in the history of American liberty.

The changed situation is reflected in nothing more dramatically than in the changed status of the men and women who work in libraries. Fifty years ago no one would have questioned the assertion that the fundamental qualification of the librarian is objectivity: fifty years ago most librarians were objective—and looked it. But when, in February of this year, Mr. Quincy Mumford, the Librarian of Congress, laid down objectivity as the prime requirement of a Library employee, there was an immediate and sharp reaction which, because of the circumstances surrounding the statement, had repercussions in the press. Dr. Albert Sprague Coolidge, son of the Library's greatest private benefactor, Mrs. Elizabeth Sprague Coolidge, had been invited by the Library to serve on the advisory committee for the Coolidge Foundation but had subsequently been passed over. In explaining the reasons for this curious sequence of events, the official *Information Bulletin* of the Library of Congress stated in its issue of February 6 that "The Librarian felt that Dr. Coolidge's past associations and activities, entirely aside from the 'loyalty' or 'security' issue, would impair that objectivity in the fulfillment of his duties that one has a right to expect of a public employee, even in an advisory capacity on cultural matters."

Made by a less distinguished librarian than Mr. Mumford and in a case of less importance than that of Dr. Coolidge, this would not perhaps have been regarded by anyone as a particularly remarkable statement. Made in the circumstances in which it was made and by the man who made it, it was felt to be remarkable indeed. And obviously it was, for what it clearly implied was that a man is not suitable for work in a library who has taken sides on controversial issues. There was, as Mr. Mumford went out of his way to state, and as those who have been associated with Dr. Coolidge well knew, no question whatever of disloyalty. Dr. Coolidge had been an effective and outspoken anti-Communist and anti-authoritarian all his life and Mr. Mumford was fully aware of that fact: "Dr. Coolidge," the *Bulletin* says, "has not been labelled a security risk by the Library of Congress either in private or in public." What was wrong was merely that Dr. Coolidge had joined organizations and taken positions which lined him up to be counted on one side—what men who love freedom would generally regard as the right side—of controversial public issues.

Now I have the greatest respect for Mr. Mumford. He came to the Library of Congress originally on my invitation: to head the new Processing Department following the reorganization of the Library in 1940 and 1941. I know at first hand his devotion, his intelligence and his professional skill. I have not the slightest doubt that he acted reluctantly in the Coolidge matter and that the step he took was the step he believed right. Nevertheless I cannot help wondering whether he fully considered the implications of his reasoning and above all whether he related it to the actual, present situation of the profession he leads. That his ruling would automatically exclude at least one former Librarian of Congress from the Library's service in the future is doubtless irrelevant and in any event immaterial since that Librarian is very fully and happily employed elsewhere. But it is not irrelevant and it is not immaterial that the statement as it stands would exclude a great many others including many of the most respected librarians in the country. No librarian who believes in the freedom guaranteed by the Constitution, and who detests authoritarianism, can avoid taking positions on controversial issues—indeed on the most controversial of all issues: for the issue of the freedom of the mind in America today is precisely that. He must believe in that freedom or he cannot be an honest librarian, and, if he believes in it, and acts on his belief, he can hardly hope to avoid contention. He may avoid such associations as Dr. Coolidge seems to have engaged in but he cannot avoid decision.

And whenever he decides that a book which somebody wants suppressed shall not be suppressed, whenever he decides that a magazine which somebody wants discontinued shall not be discontinued, he will have ceased to be "objective." He will have taken sides. He will have become a controversial figure, and as such will no longer be a desirable employee under the Librarian's rule.

I am completely certain that Mr. Mumford intended no such consequence. He knows, as any man must know who has that great institution in his charge, that the Library of Congress is the custodian of something more than a large number of books and pamphlets, maps and manuscripts. It is the custodian also of the cultural conscience of the federal government, and its actions, though they may be little noticed at the time, have enduring consequences. Had Herbert Putnam and his predecessors not accomplished the still inexplicable miracle of turning a modest legislative library into the national library of the United States, Washington would be a very different city and the federal government a very different government. Had Elizabeth Sprague Coolidge never given the Library of Congress its Coolidge Auditorium and made possible the magnificent concerts of music, new as well as old, which the Auditorium provides—had the Archive of American Folksong never been established in the Library's Music Division—the history of American music would have been a very different history. It is quite inconceivable that such an institution should now revert to a doctrine of library management, and therefore of library function, which seeks to neutralize belief and courage. The gelded librarian is a sacrifice which only McCarthyism demands and McCarthyism in decay need not now be handed its dearest victim.

Rather, the whole energy of the profession should

be directed in the opposite sense. Librarians should be encouraged to despise objectivity when objectivity means neutrality and neutrality when neutrality interferes with the performance of their duties as librarians. They should be encouraged to believe positively and combatively in those principles of a free society in which they must believe to keep their libraries whole and sane. They should be brought to see that you cannot keep an even hand, a neutral hand, between right and wrong in the running of a library in a country and a time like ours. There are certain issues as to which objectivity, if objectivity means unwillingness to take a positive position, to stand up and be counted, is impossible to a decent man in a critical period, and the issue of human freedom is one of them. You cannot be neutral on that issue anywhere in the world we live in and least of all can you be neutral on it in a library. You are for it or you are against it and if you are silent you are against. The test of a man's fitness for service in a library in the United States today is not, therefore, his lack of opinions or his failure to declare them. It is the *kind* of opinions he holds and the courage with which he makes them known. If you believe in the use of books to indoctrinate — which is to say, in the suppression of certain books in order to leave available only the views expressed in certain others — you have no place in an American library however well fitted you may be for service in a library in Czechoslovakia or Spain. If you believe in free and equal access to all substantial books regardless of their views, and if you are willing to assert your belief in words and to defend it in action, the profession, if you are otherwise qualified, should welcome you.

And it is my conviction that it will. I do not believe that American libraries will adopt the rule laid down, or seemingly laid down, in the Coolidge case.

The word, "objectivity," is, of course, a tempting word. It seems to offer a respectable way of disposing of a troublesome problem without quite facing it. "Objectivity" is one of the *good* words of our contemporary vocabulary. Scientists are objective about their findings. Judges are objective in their opinions. Great newspapers are distinguished from newspapers which call themselves great by the objectivity of their presentation of the news. When we are referred to as objective we are pleased and when we refer to others in the same terms we mean to compliment them. The word raises a standard to which our scientifically minded generation can repair as the men of the Nineties repaired to "passion" and the men of the Eighteenth Century to "sensibility." But like all *good* words "objectivity" has another side and American librarians know it. It connotes a quality—a suppression of personal commitment and personal feeling—which is admirable in a journalist reporting the news or a scientist observing an experiment or a judge judging a case, but which is anything but admirable when there is a cause to defend or a battle to be fought. A general who was objective about the outcome of a campaign might be a great military technician but he would be a soldier of limited usefulness. And a librarian who was objective about the survival of the tradition of free inquiry on which western civilization is founded might be an admira ble administrator but his services to the human spirit in a place and time like ours would be negligible or worse.

The great American libraries have given courageous proof over the past few years that this kind of objectivity does not tempt them. And the Library of Congress itself, I feel certain, has no real intention of deserting the principle. Indeed, I have good reasons for believing that the Library of Congress regards itself as still standing firm in the faith despite the unfortunate language of its statement of policy in the Coolidge case. The Library of Congress, I am reliably informed, used the word, "objectivity" in that ruling as a synonym for "good judgment" (a tribute to the influence of the scientists in our society) meaning no more than that a man who would join the organizations Sprague Coolidge had joined could not be counted on to exercise discrimination in advising the Library on the music to be played at Sprague Coolidge's mother's concerts and similar matters. If this is so the position should perhaps be clarified. Good judgment is a desirable characteristic in a library employee as in any one else—though it may well be doubted whether the soundness of a man's aesthetic sense can be determined by the orthodoxy of his political affiliations: if it could, few of the great artists and writers and musicians who have provided the contents of our libraries and museums would be employable in their management. But sound judgment as a euphuism for an unwillingness to take sides on fundamental moral and intellectual issues is not desirable anywhere in a free society and least of all in the libraries which house its memory and its conscience.

One cannot be objective in that sense and be the champion of a cause, and every American librarian worthy of the name is today the champion of a cause. It is, to my mind, the noblest of all causes for it is the cause of man, or more precisely the cause of the inquiring mind by which man has come to be. But noblest or not, it is nevertheless a cause—a struggle—not yet won: a struggle which can never perhaps be won for good and all. There are always in any society, even a society founded in the love of freedom, men and women who do not wish to be free themselves and who fear the practice of freedom by others—men and women who long for the comfort of a spiritual and intellectual authority in their own lives and who would feel more comfortable still if they could also impose such an authority on the lives of their neighbors. As long as such people exist – and they show no sign of disappearing from the earth, even the American earth – the fight to subvert freedom will continue. And as long as the fight to subvert freedom continues, libraries must be strong points of defense.

It is not as a strong point that we regard this peaceful building on the day of its dedication. But it is one notwithstanding, and will continue to be one for a long, long time to come. Young men and women will find defenses for the freedom of the mind in this place by finding here what freedom of the mind can mean. And a whole countryside will know that one more tower has been raised against ignorance and bigotry and fear: a tower which will not yield. That dedication is in the stones themselves. We do no more than name it.

The knowable and the known · 1965

Thirty years ago, when Mr. Roosevelt informed me of my desire to be Librarian of Congress, I thought I knew what a library was: it was the last place a writer ought to be found until he was stone cold on the page in print. I used to think of John Donne as I heard the early morning janitors carting the jangling brass spittoons across the marble floors on their double-decker dollies to be flushed and buffed for yet another learned day. Never ask for whom the bell tolls — you may find out.

But things have happened to the world in the last thirty years and not least to the world's libraries — particularly the great libraries and more particularly still the great libraries which serve the work of science. They have been swept from their respectable positions on the periphery of things, where they once sat back behind their Carnegie marble fronts waiting to receive the customers if and when they came. They have been swept away to find themselves at the crossroads of the time.

Ours, as we all know and constantly remind ourselves, is a revolutionary epoch. But it is not a revolutionary epoch in the political sense only, or the economic or even the technological. The turmoil

Address delivered at the dedication of the Francis A. Countway Library of Medicine, Boston, 27 May 1965. First published in Archibald MacLeish, *A Continuing Journey* (Boston: Houghton Mifflin, 1967), p.242–49.

with us goes far deeper—goes indeed to the roots of our human lives—to what is most human in our human lives—to the process of human knowledge, of human knowing itself. And it is there, of course, that the libraries are involved. For the ultimate question now is not the question whether this political order or that will prevail, or when technology will take us to the moon, or how cancer is to be conquered. The ultimate question is whether we can *know* the knowledge we have now accumulated.

Man has become at last what our remote forefathers dreamed he might become: the thief of fire. He has gone farther into the darkness than the boldest of his ancestors ever dared to hope that he might go. And what he has found, what he has brought back again, is what Prometheus found: not only the precious ember glowing in its secret pith but a destiny also—the challenge to the gods which is a challenge to himself: the challenge of knowledge. If we can inflict death as the gods in their immense catastrophes inflict it (and we already have)—if we can create life from acids and from sunlight as the gods create it (and there are those who think we may)—then the question will present itself whether we can also know as the gods know . . .

And, if we can, if we can stand it.

It may not be in the great scientific libraries that this question will be answered—the question whether mankind can bear to know *as knowledge* what hitherto we have known only as faith—but it is almost certainly there or thereabouts that a beginning will be made at the answering of that other earlier question: not whether we can bear to know this new knowledge of ours in all its frightening implications but whether we can know it in its entirety at all.

Pierre Auger's calculation that 90 per cent of all the scientists who ever lived are alive today is sometimes taken as a tribute to progress, a compliment to the generation. Actually it has a different sense. It measures the immeasurable rapidity with which the flood of scientific discovery has inundated our age. Most of the revolutionary advances which have changed the world — or changed, at least, our human relation to the world — have taken place within the memories of men now living.

And within that same time, science itself has changed, grown, proliferated, multiplied. What was once a single discipline or family of disciplines — Physics, Biology, Chemistry, Geology — has become a society of nations speaking as many different tongues as there are territories in which to use them. A few years ago Sir Charles Snow set the academic world to arguing about the two cultures, by which he apparently meant the two languages of the humanities and the natural sciences. But as time passed and the debate went on it became clearer and clearer that there were not two languages but many more than two and that the scientists had quite as much trouble understanding each other as the rest of us had in understanding them. "Learned societies," said Lord Ritchie-Calder of Edinburgh University, "themselves splinter groups of natural philosophy, have sub-groups within groups and sub-sections within sections" to such a point that "it is questionable whether anyone or any body has ever made a complete list of all the so-called branches of science," and the consequence, he goes on, is that we have "narrower and narrower briefings in the fluorescent glare of seminar and colloquia where, in their private jargon, the scientists discuss last week's meson, the latest amino-acid synthesis or a hair on the whisker of the banana fly."

What Lord Ritchie-Calder was talking about was the effect of all this on science: the burgeoning babel, the increasing fragmentation. But there is another consequence far more serious: the effect on human knowledge itself—on the techniques for making that knowledge available, making it *known* at the time and place where it is needed. Prior to the beginning of the great proliferation, when those techniques were in process of development in the principal libraries of the world, human knowledge was a common human possession, the common inheritance of educated men. Few, perhaps, were masters of it all but from no part or province was any educated mind excluded. The Royal Society can be traced back to Comenius' proposal of an international college where the wise of the world were to meet to examine together and make universally known the whole body of natural knowledge, and it was still possible at the beginning of the nineteenth century for learned societies to hear famous engineers arguing music with professional astronomers and chemists debating political philosophy with biologists while obstetricians lectured judges on the caesura not in the female abdomen but in a line of verse.

The knowable, at that point, differed from the known only in terms of time and labor—the time and labor required for reference and reading—and the function of the librarian was merely to provide the tools and facilities which would make the search brief and the reading comfortable. But now, within a century or less, all this has changed. It is no longer true, if we are to believe the scientists themselves, that knowledge is whole—that what is known to one mind is necessarily knowable to another and therefore part and parcel of a common knowledge. Robert Oppenheimer is reported to have dismissed the Snow complaint about the failure of humanists to study physics with the remark that it didn't really matter whether they did or not since no one but the modern physicist can understand modern physics anyway. And the same thing can apparently be said, whether it has been or not, of the rest of the modern sciences, or, in any case, of the languages in which they express themselves. The commonly known, or, more precisely, the commonly knowable, no longer includes the growing edge of science, the new frontiers of experiment and discovery where the future of mankind is being made. That is specialists' country which one man or a dozen can enter but not more — not the rest of us — not the ordinary educated man.

What this has done to the universities is a familiar story. No longer able to assume that a disciplined mind will enable a man to travel anywhere, the makers of curricula have invented courses, commonly called courses in General Education, which take account of the intellectual fragmentation of our world. Apprentice physicists are led back into the old heart-land of the humanities for a tour of the more memorable sites while apprentice scholars or lawyers or businessmen or writers are taken up upon a temporary mountain from which they can just make out the distant, unplowed, scientific country where the dust begins. It is a pleasant journey in both directions but not always a productive one. The apprentice scholars still remain apprentice scholars with a vague and uncomfortable memory of something glimpsed they have no wish to glimpse again and the apprentice scientists, though they may loaf among the olives for a while, can hardly wait to head their horses west.

But what creates difficulties for the teachers creates impossibilities for the librarians. The mere existence of a library collection, as distinguished from a warehouse full of printed pages, presupposes the intellectual coherence of the materials collected. Books can be brought together according to an organization, a classification of one kind or another, only if what they *contain* composes an organization — composes, that is to say, a whole of which no part is foreign to any other part. All, it must be assumed, have come from the human mind and all are therefore parts of human knowledge, and human knowledge, by hypothesis, is one — one because the human mind can hold it.

When that hypothesis breaks down, when human knowledge is no longer one because the human mind can no longer hold it, when there are parts — essential parts — of human knowledge which are not knowable at all to the vast majority of human minds, the library is in trouble. It can no longer perform its function of making the knowable known at the time and place where it is needed by merely possessing classified and catalogued collections and providing space for their use. It must intervene actively in the increasingly difficult process of knowing, preparing itself when necessary to mediate between the human mind and those who have — or think they have — outdistanced it; undertaking, if not to translate the untranslatable knowledge of those scientists Oppenheimer had in mind, at least to place it in its spectrum, so that what we cannot *know*, we can know *of*.

The significance — the historic significance — of the dedication of the new library of the Harvard Medical School is precisely that this is such a library. The library of the Harvard Medical School will combine two of the best medical collections in the world to form a total collection of about three quarters of a million volumes rich with rare and irreplaceable books — the Streeter bequest and many others. It will be housed in a handsome and efficient building designed specifically to meet its needs. It will be associated with the other great medical libraries of the area in a communications net which will make the resources of all available for the needs of any one. But none of this is as important, either for the library itself or for the society in which it exists, as the fact that this new library proposes to use its human and intellectual resources, which include the human and intellectual resources of the greatest medical school in the Republic and those of the university to which that school belongs, to perform a positive function in what its librarian calls "the handling and communication of scientific *information*." No longer will this library limit itself to the great custodial and reference tasks which have occupied librarians in the past: keeping the collection up and in order, perfecting the catalogues, leading the readers to the books. In addition it will play an active part in the process of the dissemination of information, attempting to develop means to carry the new knowledge in the sciences related to medicine directly to the working doctors throughout the area who need it.

If the effort succeeds — and who can doubt that it will — the library of the Medical School will have done something more than improve the practice of medicine in these parts, something more than enlarge the function of the scholarly library. It will have connected the republic of common knowledge with parts at least of that revolutionary frontier which so often seems to turn its back, like all frontiers, on the peopled lands behind it.

And this will be no accidental or unintended consequence. In the new library there is to be a room of a kind not ordinarily found in scientific libraries — a room without a scientific book on its shelves but poetry instead, music, history, art. This room will be called the Aesculapian Room, dedicated thus to the god of medicine and healing. Why is it this room which is so called? Why not the others with their shelves full of physiology and anatomy and biochemistry and the rest? Because the library recognizes, as Harvard herself, I think, has always recognized, that there is no such thing as knowledge by itself but only knowledge *to* the knower, and that the knower is never anything but man, man in his old condition as man, man with his wonder on him, his poetry, his music. Because the library recognizes, as Harvard recognizes, that the god is in the question, not the answer. Because the library recognizes, as the university recognizes, that it is only when the answer is responsive to the question, when the science has been mastered by the man, that civilization is possible.

Changes
in the ritual of library
dedication · 1967

A man who dedicates two libraries
in the same town in a single decade is
entitled to reflect on the phenomenon of library
dedication, and I have done so. With the result that
I have reached one firm conclusion: nothing in this
age of unexampled change has changed as much as
the process and procedures by which institutions of
this character get themselves opened to the public.

Thirty years ago or 40 or 50 or 150, the dedication
of a public library was an act of civic piety to be celebrated with lemonade, parasols, and an address by
some suitable dignitary in which the community
was congratulated on the substantial architectural
proof of its cultural maturity and the visible indication that it had surpassed the literary pretensions of
any town in the neighborhood, with the possible
exception of Cambridge.

What mattered in those far-off, happy, by-gone
days was the building, not the books. It was assumed as a matter of course, that all books were
respectable if not indeed uplifting, that their possession was more significant than their use, that the
principal duty of librarians was to keep them on the
shelves, or at least get them back to the shelves as

Address delivered at the dedication of the Wallace Library,
Fitchburg, Mass., 3 June 1967. Reprinted from *Library Journal*
93:3517–20 (1 October 1968), published by R. R. Bowker Co. (a
Xerox company), © 1968 by R. R. Bowker Co.

promptly and neatly as possible, and that their readers, if there had to be readers, would be either the very young on their way, like Abraham Lincoln and Andrew Carnegie, to fame and fortune with the help of great examples, or the very old who had nothing to do anyway. Gamey books, handed down from earlier generations (which hadn't thought of them as gamey) were kept in a locked drawer in the librarian's desk marked "Delta Collection," and volumes of revolutionary speculation, economic, philosophical, and political, were shelved alphabetically with the rest since it had never occurred to anyone in that epoch that the American people could not be trusted to read unorthodox opinions and make up their minds about them for themselves.

All of us over 30 — if there are any of us left who are willing to admit to being over 30 — remember libraries such as those: high-ceiled caves of quiet, enormous empty rooms where you could sit on summer mornings and hear the flies buzz louder than the occasional cars outside; musty stackrooms where the ancient air still smelled of leather bindings because there still were leather bindings. Sometimes — perhaps more often than we think — such libraries served a purpose: young Bob Linscott at the table by the window who used his 20¢ for carfare, not for lunch, and kept on coming day by day until he had taught himself the English poets, and then learned French and read Racine, and so became an editor at Houghton Mifflin . . . young Bob Linscott or the old, stiff, half-blind lady at the table on the other side who borrowed the same novel every day until she read through, and then reread it, year by year, until at last she'd finished reading. Such things happened, but not always — not even often. For the most part, libraries before the wars were large, vague, almost empty buildings under huge, still living elms which no one thought of much except as landmarks.

To dedicate a library in those days was to dedicate—rededicate—the past: to say the obvious and
eat your chicken salad and go home. But then, in the
late forties, all this changed. The United States, having won triumphantly the greatest of all wars, found
itself suddenly and inexplicably afraid. It had vanquished its enemies only to find it hadn't vanquished
all its enemies, and suddenly and for no rational
reason, it had lost its nerve. When a totally incon-
siderable Senator from a middle-western state
announced that a vital department of the federal
government was rotten with traitors, millions of
Americans, though he offered no proof, believed him.
The country began to doubt itself. It ceased to believe
in its own integrity, its own good faith, the loyalty of
its own people. Even the fundamental proposition on
which it had been founded, the belief in freedom,
the belief in the right of a free man to think for himself and decide for himself, became suspect. Congressional committees began to investigate the opinions of citizens, newspaper persecutions followed,
blacklists were established in various industries,
men and women were hounded out of their jobs and
out of their communities—even out of their lives;
and for a period not of months but years the first
wholly free society ever founded on this earth lived
in a shameful panic, a discreditable unfaithfulness
to itself, a cowardly betrayal of its most profound
convictions.

In those years, naturally enough, libraries
changed and the dedication of libraries changed
with them. A frightened government which claimed
the right to investigate opinions and to punish ideas
necessarily claimed the right to censor and suppress
books, and to censor and suppress books is to control
and regulate libraries. Thus the dedication of a new
library in the long years before the Senate sum-
moned the courage to rebuke McCarthy and bring

the country to its senses was anything but a peaceful act of self-congratulation and quiet pride. It was
an act of defiance and protest—defiance not of a
demogogue in Congress alone but of the whole mias-
ma of suspicion and censorship and fear he had let
loose on the country: the women's organization in
Chicago which proposed to tell the American people
what they could and could not read; the police officers and vigilantes in towns and cities throughout the
country who blackmailed bookstores to suppress
books *they* disapproved of; the members of the Massachusetts legislature who drafted a bill to authorize
the Attorney General to tell publishers what was
publishable in Massachusetts; the innumerable self-
appointed committees in every state who arrogated
to themselves the right to decide for their neighbors
what books the public libraries could own.

To dedicate a new library under these circumstances was to denounce this fearfulness, to reassert
a confidence in mankind in general and in the American people in particular, to commit one's self again
to the old high hope in a government of the people
and *by* the people in which the *people* read the
books they wished to read and held the opinions they
chose to hold—in which the *people*, not a member of
Congress, not a church organization, not the chief of
the local police, not a committee of the neighbors—
even the nicest neighbors—but the *people*, the people *themselves*, made up their minds for themselves,
governed their country for themselves, and respected in each other the freedom of mind and of word
the Republic was founded to insure.

The dedication of a library in those disgraceful
years was, in other words, an act of war, an act in
the ancient, the original, war to establish and to defend the kind of free society the American constitution contemplated—an act in the endless and unceasing war which will never be won so long as

there are Americans who do not believe in that America, men who support a [Joseph] McCarthy or join a John Birch Society or meet in secret with the Minutemen or march in parades for Power—White Power or Black Power or any other kind.

It would be a mistake, perhaps, to say that American libraries, those arsenals of the weapons of intellectual freedom played a principal part in the debunking of McCarthyism, but it would be only just to add that many of the most authentic heroes of that desperate campaign were librarians notwithstanding—underpaid and often isolated men and women in villages and towns and suburbs, even cities, even cities in enlightened states, who refused as a matter of principle to be bullied by the local vigilantes and who demonstrated, sometimes at the cost of their livelihood and of more than their livelihood, a passionate loyalty to the American idea of freedom—the freedom of free men and women to do their reading for themselves.

That was one change in the ritual of dedication—a change which, in retrospect, left certain benefits behind—unintended benefits but benefits none the less. During the McCarthy persecutions the emphasis in the dedication of a library shifted from the building to the books: it was the books you fought for because it was the books that were under attack. With the result that books began to matter on both sides: to the censors and suppressors because some books were dangerous—or dangerous at least to them; to the liberators and believers because some books had been condemned by extra-legal process and all books were thereby opened to extralegal condemnation. Censorship, which had been a minor issue, of interest only to prudes and pornographers, became, in the wake of McCarthyism, a major concern to society as a whole. If you could take *Lolita* off the shelves by mob action in the Congress or out of it, you could take Marx off the shelves, and if you could take Marx off the shelves Thoreau could follow, and if Thoreau followed what was to prevent the emasculation of the collection by the removal of Jefferson or any other political writer of whom the old ladies of Los Angeles, or the chairman of a Senate Committee, or some so-called patriotic secret society disapproved? More and more Americans, taught by those wretched years, came to see that the only true security for a self-governing nation was confidence in its own self-government—confidence in the people—confidence in the ability of the people to make up their minds for themselves, to determine the facts for themselves, to think their thoughts for themselves, to decide for themselves what they would read, what they would decide, how they would act. The people, as Mr. Lincoln observed, may be fooled part of the time, but no one who lived through the fifties will doubt that, even so, they are far less apt to be foolish than the innumerable volunteers in Congress and out, who offer to do their thinking for them.

A second change in the ritual of dedication, involving a second change in the idea of the library, has occurred in our own decade—or perhaps I should say, has made itself felt in that decade, for its origins lie back in the beginnings of the electronic revolution 30 years ago. The electronic revolution altered the human role in the terrestrial drama, promoting man from his aboriginal place at the back end of a spear or the working end of a shovel or the controls of a machine to his new place as the master of electricity—of automation. Not only do contraptions of one sort or another do the greater part of his work for him: they also perform an important part of his thinking. But they perform these functions only at his commands and under his instructions. Even a computer must be programmed first. Before it can forecast within a tolerance of three tenths of one percent the presidential vote in the state of New Hampshire, it must first be supplied with the 1968 vote in the town of Gull, the 1964 vote in the same town, the average discrepancy over the last three campaigns between the editorial forecasts of the New Hampshire press and the verdict of history, an extrapolation of tendencies in the town of Gull as compared with tendencies in the County of Webster, and an overall résumé of the political sophistication of the people of the southeastern counties since the Spanish War.

All this, of course, requires information. And the result has been that the reservoirs of information, of which the library is naturally the greatest, have assumed a new and overwhelming importance in human life: an importance so great that the storage and supply of information have begun to seem — and not to poll watchers alone — the principal functions of libraries in the electronic world. Terms like "retrieval" take the place of the old word, "reference": you no longer "refer" a reader to a book, you "retrieve" the information he wants from the periodical collections and microfilm boxes. Computer tapes are distributed to research libraries throughout the country, giving them access to the contents of every new English-language monograph cataloged by the Library of Congress, and sooner or later the entire Library of Congress catalog will itself be made available on tape. At M.I.T., 60,000 bibliographic citations from 17 physics journals have been fed into a computer, and the information thus stored made available to researchers near and far by teletype machines connected directly to the electronic source.

And so it goes. When I became Librarian of Congress in 1939, my properly puzzled little daughter wanted to know if daddy was going to "give out the books." Today no one, not even a properly puzzled little daughter, would ask that question. Books are no longer the librarian's commodity; it is the information *in* the books that matters. When Marshall McLuhan, the Mohammed of the electronic age, emits his slogan, "The medium is the message," he merely carries the process to its logical conclusion. If information is the end and aim, then the fact that information can be electronically disseminated, instantaneously communicated from one end of the earth to the other, is itself perhaps the most important piece of information one can have. For if information is the end and aim, it makes little difference what the particular bit of information is. All that matters is the fact that one has been informed.

All this, like the earlier events which changed the notion of a library from building to books, has its advantages from certain points of view. For one thing, it assures the librarian of an importance he never had—or at least was never recognized as having—in the old quaint world of print and paper. The managing editor of the *New York Daily News*, a publication not previously distinguished for its interest in librarians, is quoted as having told the Special Libraries Association that "no newspaperman will be more important than the librarian of the future"—a generous reassurance if ever there was one. And certainly the electronic, computerized library of the future will not need to bow to anyone, even the *Daily News*. It will be an essential part, arguably *the* essential part, of the new and sophisticated system by which humanity will perform its neo-human function of feeding information to machines. Indeed, in certain particular instances as, for example, the magnificent new library of the Harvard Medical School, the library will be more than that: it will itself direct and operate the system, determining, by means of its own scholarly resources in the Medical School and the University, what information will be most important to the doctors and clinics and hospitals it serves, and, where necessary, instigating the production and discovery of new and needed information not previously available.

But admirable as these miraculous electronic contraptions are, they nevertheless raise certain questions. For the fact is, of course, that these new facilities for the dissemination of information become available precisely at a time when the great human need is not for additional information or more rapid information or more universally available information but for the comprehension of the enormous quantities of existing information the scientific and other triumphs of the last several generations have already dumped into our minds. It is not additional "messages" we need, and least of all additional "messages" which merely tell us that the medium which communicates the message has changed the world. We know the world has changed and is daily changing—changing more rapidly and radically than it has ever changed before. What we do not know is *how*, precisely, it is changing and in what direction and with what consequences to ourselves.

The urgent question with us, in other words, is not the question of how or the question of what: it is the question of who. Who are we? It is the question of why. Why are we here? To what end? Is there an end or is human life a tragic absurdity, a meaningless jape? The whole, huge restlessness underlying our literature, our art, is a reverberation of that question.

It is not ignorance—lack of information—which has shaken our souls: it is knowledge, sudden (however partial) knowledge, vast floods of unassimilated, uncomprehended knowledge. We know enough about the universe to see how small a part we play on this infinitesimal planet circling this tiny star at the edge of a trifling galaxy among immeasurably larger galaxies. We have looked far enough into the sky to realize there is no heaven there: deep enough into the mysteries of matter to discern a tremendous structure soaring out beyond our capacities of comprehension into space and time. We understand as no generation of humanity has ever understood before that men do truly die and yet we do not understand our deaths. We realize, as men in earlier generations could not realize, the psychological complications of our selves and yet our selves escape us: we know far less about our human nature than the Greeks. And the consequence is that our philosophy has collapsed, our religions are shaken, and our arts live face to face with anguish and despair. "Information" has given us the affluent society and the affluent society has polluted the earth, alienated its children, corrupted its cities, and run mad in meaningless, murderous, unmentionable wars. Leaving that naked question: Who am I? What is man? — the one question "information" never answers but can only ask — the one question the electronic library of "information" can only put to its computers — not resolve.

But who can answer it then — and where? In the new Countway Library of the Harvard Medical School, there is an Aesculapian Room, a room sacred to the god of medicine and healing. In that room there is not one scientific book, not one monograph on any technical or technological topic. Instead there are books of poetry, books of high literature, books which hold the long and anxious record of man's unceasing search for knowledge of himself, his life, his death. Why are those books there at the center of that library? In the judgment of Harvard University, because they belong there: because the question comes before the answer; because the man comes first before the information. And so of course he does.

And so, and for the same reason does the general library which continues to concern itself with literature and with works of art and mind belong at the center of the vast new electronic society which exists for science and for progress and for the new brave world.